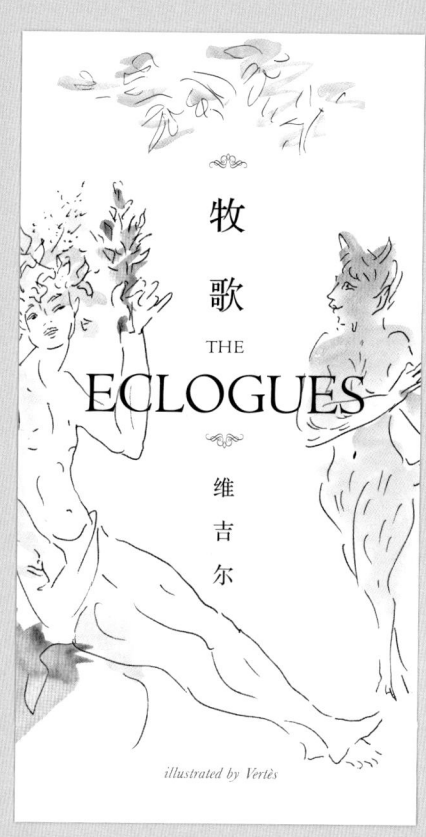

牧 歌

○● 插图珍藏版 × 汉英对照 ○●

THE ECLOGUES

[古罗马]
维吉尔
著

[法] 马塞尔·韦尔特 —— 绘　[英] C. S. 卡尔弗利 —— 英译　叶紫 —— 译

江苏凤凰文艺出版社
JIANGSU PHOENIX LITERATURE AND ART PUBLISHING

图书在版编目（CIP）数据

牧歌：插图珍藏版：汉英对照 /（古罗马）维吉尔著；（法）马塞尔·韦尔特绘；（英）C.S.卡尔弗利英译；叶紫译. -- 南京：江苏凤凰文艺出版社，2021.8
ISBN 978-7-5594-5875-9

Ⅰ.①牧… Ⅱ.①维…②马…③C…④叶… Ⅲ.①英语-汉语-对照读物②诗集-古罗马 Ⅳ.①H319.4：Ⅰ

中国版本图书馆CIP数据核字(2021)第082045号

牧歌（插图珍藏版）

[古罗马]维吉尔 著　　[法]马塞尔·韦尔特 绘　　[英]C.S.卡尔弗利 英译　叶紫 译

策　　划	尚　飞
责任编辑	李龙姣
特约编辑	陈怡萍
装帧设计	墨白空间·肖雅
出版发行	江苏凤凰文艺出版社
	南京市中央路165号，邮编：210009
网　　址	http://www.jswenyi.com
印　　刷	南京爱德印刷有限公司
开　　本	889毫米×1194毫米　1/16
印　　张	9.75
字　　数	83千字
版　　次	2021年8月第1版
印　　次	2021年8月第1次印刷
书　　号	ISBN 978-7-5594-5875-9
定　　价	118.00元

江苏凤凰文艺版图书凡印刷、装订错误，可向出版社调换，联系电话 025 - 83280257

目录

1
导读　by 摩西·豪道什

19
导读注释

牧歌 / THE ECLOGUES

23
其一 / ECLOGUE Ⅰ

35
其二 / ECLOGUE Ⅱ

45
其三 / ECLOGUE Ⅲ

63
其四 / ECLOGUE Ⅳ

73
其五 / ECLOGUE V

87
其六 / ECLOGUE VI

99
其七 / ECLOGUE VII

109
其八 / ECLOGUE VIII

125
其九 / ECLOGUE IX

135
其十 / ECLOGUE X

145
注释

导读

by 摩西·豪道什[1]

1

对现代读者而言，在所有曾经风行一时的诗歌形式中，田园牧歌无疑是最陌生的一种。这不仅仅是说，夸张的艺术技巧，一如女性时尚领域中的奇思妙想，会迅速过时，也不仅仅是说，艺术形式会被时间淘汰：时至今日，荷马史诗、古希腊悲剧，甚至品达[2]的颂歌——这些年代更为久远，技巧更为复杂、精密的作品——依然被人们当作诗歌而非纯粹的"古董"来诵读。不同于其他诗歌形式的是，在田园牧歌中，由于艺术手段与艺术目的在某种程度上并不协调（并非"均衡"不足，而是"音调"有别），"技巧"往往会成为一种由外而内的"入侵"。

这种不协调性之所以存在，大概是因为田园牧歌不是一种源于前人所成，逐渐发展而来的诗歌形式，而是一种发明创造。史诗与悲剧迈向成熟之前所经历的各个发展阶段都有迹可循，或者说，这些阶段似乎可以逐步得到合理的推定，而牧歌却仿佛是由忒奥克里图斯[3]凭空捏造而成，突然问世于公元前三世纪上半叶的新奇事物。但事实上，没有任何一种文学形式能像从宙斯的脑袋里一跃而出的雅典娜一般突然降生，而且生来成熟。就像众多承其衣钵的田园诗人一样，忒奥克里图斯本人也是一位自觉的，深受文学传统熏陶的文人。也许，在对有可能曾为忒奥克里图斯的作品提供"胚种"的前人之作略加审视之后，人们便可明辨忒式田园诗的优越之处与不足之处。

在所有可能对忒式田园诗造成过影响的古老文学体裁中，有此三种体裁——即滑稽剧（mime）、乌托邦传奇（utopian romance）和赞美诗（hymn）——具备了一些独特的品质：似乎正是这些品质，决定了忒式田园诗的特质。"滑稽剧"是最易识别的源头，因为与忒奥克里图斯的田园诗一样，"滑稽剧"起用虚构的角色，以对话的形式展开，而且通常都具备"西西里式"的背景设定。"滑稽剧"是一个统称，涵盖了众多类型的创作。从广义上讲，各种各样单独表演的艺人（包括歌手、舞者、杂耍艺人、魔术师、哑剧演员）——无论他们是否曾在宴会或者市集上展示过技艺——都被希腊人称作"滑稽演员"，而文学则只与那些扮演着某种有趣的角色，高声朗诵段段独白，一心想通过言语和举止来达成戏剧效果并取悦于人的表演者相关。很有可能，以如此形式得到呈现的角色正是欧洲文学史上最原始的"虚构人物"，因为史诗与悲剧中的角色无一不是"历史性"的存在。

在某种远远超越其起源和正常发展过程的层面，柏拉图的对话录或许也能被视作一种滑稽剧本，而且，据说教会柏拉图对话体创作的，正是西西里人埃庇卡摩斯[4]。的确，西西里地区由始至终都是滑稽剧的温床，而且，它也在多利安方言密布的滑稽剧语言中留下了它的印记。西西里人索福戎[5]的滑稽剧作品曾被分成"男性剧"和"女性剧"两类，剧名皆为《农夫》（*The Peasant*）、《金枪鱼渔夫》（*The Tunny Fisher*）、《女裁缝》（*The Needle Woman*）、《女巫》（*The Sorceress*）以及《岳母》（*The Mother-in-Law*）之属。除此之外，后来也曾出现过另一种（适用于忒奥克里图斯的）分类方法，即"城市剧"和"乡村剧"之分。

到了希腊化时代，滑稽剧作者成了严肃的艺术家，均被冠以"生物学家"（biologists）或者"生命学者"（students of life）之名；任何一位开明的、欲求理解治下国民性格的托勒密王族成员都会被建议去听听"生物学家"们的说法。赫伦达斯[6]留存至今的滑稽剧作品足以证明"生物学家"并非虚名，而忒奥克里图斯的田园诗第十五——《阿多尼斯节上的女人》(*The Women at the Festival of Adonis*)——在极大程度上也堪称一部生物学著作。此外，忒奥克里图斯的其他田园诗作都保留着某种真正意义上的滑稽剧特质，但在大多数篇目中，"生物学"元素已为纯粹的田园元素所取代。忒式田园诗实际上是一种全新的诗歌体裁；其中的人物并非"角色"，人物之间的对唱也并非"对话"。尽可能独立于现实之外的想象正是田园诗的本质所在。

田园诗人所创造的，是属于他自己的世界。正是在这层意义上，他所采用的技巧才能成为高度严肃的技巧。田园诗人鄙弃世俗的世界，遵循内心的向往，塑造出一个与世隔绝的阿卡迪亚[7]，从而在实现最大程度的想象性创造的同时，为自己提供一处可供检验人类潜能之本性，如同一片按需搭建的试验田一般的场所。古希腊古典文学同样为此提供了范例。《奥德赛》中费阿刻斯人的领地和以阿里斯托芬[8]的《鸟》(*Birds*)为最佳代表的一系列"旧喜剧"，都展示出这片按需搭建的试验田何以可能被用来研究人性。在这一方面，田园诗的可能性或许可以朗格斯[9]的《达夫尼斯与克洛伊》(*Daphnis and Chloe*)为例来阐明；尽管是以散文体写成，问世时间也比忒奥克里图斯的田园诗晚了数个世纪，但它依然是我们所能读到的最饱满的田园诗作。在《达夫尼斯与克洛伊》中，作者坦率地承认他所创作的，是一则旨在阐释爱的运作原理的虚构故事——一份以其亲眼所见的一幅图景为主体的补充。他在一个与世隔绝的山谷中搭建起他的试验田，选定两个在情爱方面的成熟过程有待被研究的弃儿为实验对象，继而挑选并引入一系列来自外部世界的入侵者，来观察他们对整个成熟过程的影响；最终，在实验对象完全成熟之际，实验便告完结，实验对象也回归传统社会，找到自己的定位。的确，忒奥克里图斯的田园诗仅仅勾勒出田园诗的实验性可能的轮廓，但就像其他一些人文主义田园诗一样，维吉尔的"弥赛亚牧歌"(*Messianic Eclogue*)却切实地描绘出一个具有严肃意义的乌托邦。在这层意义上，当代科幻小说或许算得上是田园诗的某种略显怪异的转世。

赞美诗也许是对田园牧歌影响最大的文学体裁，尽管和滑稽剧、乌托邦传奇等相比，它更不显眼。公元前六七世纪曾经出现过一组被称为"荷马赞美诗"（Homeric Hymns）的诗作——尽管其作者并非荷马。这组诗歌旨在于侍奉重要神明的节日里为礼拜仪式所用，每一首诗都通过讲述能够体现某位特定的神明在其独特的司掌领域中具有何等超凡才能的案例，来赞美这位神明。对于在某种清教式宗教传统的熏陶下长大的人来说，一份关于阿芙洛狄忒（Aphrodite）如何引诱安喀塞斯（Anchises）或者赫尔墨斯（Hermes）如何施展惊人骗术的描述很难被想象成某种宗教仪式的组成部分，但如果爱与机智正是圆满人生的基本要素，那么通过颂扬这种超凡的爱与机智来赞美司掌爱与机智的神明，也就无可指摘了。

《致德墨忒尔》（*To Demeter*）无疑是赞美诗中最精彩的一首。它讲述了哈迪斯（Hades）如何掳走珀耳塞福涅（Persephone），珀母德墨忒尔如何在伊洛西斯（Eleusis）通过悉心照料一个人类男婴来抚平心中的伤痛，如何以饥荒来向天神与人类复仇，终又如何让女儿在每年作物生长期间留在自己身边，也讲述了旨在纪念她的悲伤与妥协的"伊洛西斯秘仪"（Eleusinian Mysteries）如何得到确立。那种深邃的宗教氛围清晰可感，而且其文字之馥郁、亲切，以及人性温度与神圣威严在诗中的融合，的确极其贴近我们对于宗教的理解。然而，如果这首诗被印在一部田园假面剧集之中，它的宗教特质便可能不会受到人们的注意。一切俱在：那片熟悉的花红柳绿，那些芳名质朴的乡村姑娘，那些戴上假面，自贬身份，纵情于歌舞的名流要士，以及众人摘下面具之后在和解中响起的尾声。因此，人们不难理解，像《致德墨忒尔》这样的诗歌何以在其宗教意义逐渐退散之后，依然因其美学价值而备受珍重。

包括文学在内，许多希腊化时代的艺术的核心特质在于，它们出于纯粹的美学考量而予以发展的艺术形式自有其原始的宗教内涵，但它们显然对这些内涵无所觉察。卡利马科斯[10]的赞美诗与"荷马赞美诗"在形式上尤为相似，但前者却不带有任何真挚的宗教情感，而且，二者在传统上常被结合起来辑录一处这一事实，也足以表明在后来的希腊人看来，二者之间并不存在真正意义上的区别。让我们有能力拉长视线，将更古老的思维模式与表达模式纳入视野的"历史意识"其实是一种现代意义上的产物。亚历山大时代的文学作者就曾理所当然地认为他们所遵循的标准自古适用。如果他们的创作是"为了艺术而艺术"，那么他们便无法想象，古典文学的动机其实各不相同。在创作《阿尔戈英雄纪》（*Argonautica*）时，罗德岛人阿波罗尼俄斯[11]无疑认为，他正以精密的技艺和隐秘的素材书写荷马以其天真无邪的笔法与显而易见的素材书写的故事，不曾意识到《阿尔戈英雄纪》与荷马史诗之间的本质差异。

所以，很有可能，在着手创作田园诗时，忒奥克里图斯也类似地误解了——或者根本不曾在意过——"荷马赞美诗"（更确切地说，是《致德墨忒尔》）的真正本质。最直观的证据之一便是六步格的使用。六步格是古希腊诗歌韵律中最为庄严的一种，也是吟诵赞美诗时的不二之选，但忒奥克里图斯的田园诗里包含众多乡村歌谣。真正适合这些歌谣的，并非同一模式的宣叙调诗节，而是抒情诗的韵律形式与分节方法。"一首六步格歌谣"（a hexameter song）本身就是一种自相矛盾的说法；忒奥克里图斯的歌谣之所以"异常"，也许恰是因为这种"异常"正是在他认为他所遵循的传统中得到了确立。

他不仅在歌谣创作中采用了不恰当的韵律，更以如此韵律为基础来描述乡土人物的言行。正是这两大"异常"为我们提供了最明确的评判指标，忒诗（及其追随者的作品）的优越之处与不足之处一目了然。在古典作品中，六步格始终和真正意义上的神明与英雄的事迹保持着牢不可破的关联。在以自己的名义高声论说当代政治问题与社会问题时，梭伦[12]和忒奥格尼斯[13]都会起用庄重程度低于六步格的哀歌韵律，而且，一旦某种更为主观的"反英雄"情绪油然而生，毫无庄重可言的抑扬格便会成为它的表达模式。常规的滑稽剧韵律——比如赫伦达斯所采用的韵律——正是迥异于忒诗韵律的抑扬韵律。就总体而言，古希腊文学始于英雄文学，终于世俗文学：欧里庇得斯[14]的悲剧、"新喜剧"[15]以及散文体传奇（prose romance）是其演变过程中的三大地标。卡利马科斯和阿波罗尼俄斯的作品中确也存在六步格的使用，但它们都是有意识的"仿古"行为。《阿尔戈英雄纪》中的故事发生在英雄时代，形形色色的英雄人物是故事的主角；可实际上，伊阿宋只是亚历山大时代的一位花花公子，雅典娜与赫拉也只是亚历山大时代的两位上流社会妇女。直到五世纪，缪塞俄斯[16]才在《海洛与利安德》（*Hero and Leander*）中首次作出了旨在崇高化一则根本意义上的世俗故事的尝试。为此，他不仅以英雄格[17]韵律行文，更以英雄人物标志性的惨死来为全诗收尾。

由此我们便能理解，早在《海格与利安德》问世约八百年前，就已毫无避讳地以乡土人物为主题来创作诗歌的忒奥克里图斯，究竟作出了何等重大的创新，也能理解忒式田园诗何以在诸多方面自相矛盾。有时，比如在《收获节》（*Harvest Home*，田园诗第七）中，乡村气息浓厚的外在表现其实只是"绅士诗人"（gentlemen-poets）的伪装；有时，诗中又散发出某种贵人屈身乡野，慷慨以助穷苦的气质；有时，模糊之感始终不曾消退。可贵的是，尽管其诗作无法脱离种种为其创造本身所固有、受其所处时代之局限的人为技巧，但忒奥克里图斯是一位真正关心人与自然的诗人。他同情平凡的人性，而这份同情的基石，即是他对人类心理的精准理解；即便这份同情算不上前无古人，他对乡野之景与乡野之声的感知——那份同样饱含同情的感知——也当之无愧。

也许，这份对于自然世界的全新关注源于犬儒学派的教诲；也许，它是一种逃避亚历山大时代崇尚精致优雅的宫廷生活风的方法（在任何一座现代大都会常住的人都会受到类似的吸引）。的确，特别是在《收获节》里，那层乡村外衣假得就像扮演挤奶女工的玛丽·安托瓦内特[18]披上的伪装,但那种在夏末一个清风醉人、花香四溢的日子里尽情弥漫的轻松愉悦,却在诗中得到了无可比拟的完美呈现。如果忒奥克里图斯不是一个明明可以安享客房服务,却要赶在天亮前起床去牲口棚里打理杂务的人,那他必已清楚地看到、听到、闻到田野与牲畜的模样、声音与气息,并且不曾感到厌恶。继《底比斯战纪》(*Thebaid*)而来的一长列续作已然以其性质扭曲、"披绸挂缎"的田园诗风让我们对田园诗歌由爱转腻;其真正的缺陷在于,无论是这些作品本身,还是它们的喉舌,都从未比前辈田园诗人们的作品更贴近自然。除了满面脂粉、穿着裙撑的牧羊女之外,还有谁能和眉毛拔得整整齐齐、袖口镶着花边的牧羊人意趣相投?

然而,当严肃的意义遭到清空,诗歌形式退化成一层无足轻重的外壳,这层外壳又将背负起一种崭新的严肃。古典史诗与古典悲剧如此,田园诗也是如此。如上所述,忒奥克里图斯的田园诗隐约勾勒出种种具有严肃意义的可能,而这些可能也在以彼翁[19]的《悼阿多尼斯》(*Lament for Adonis*)、维吉尔的"弥赛亚牧歌"、斯宾塞[20]的《牧人月历》(*Shephearde's Calendar*)以及弥尔顿[21]的《利西达斯》(*Lycidas*)为代表的诸多诗作中得到了实现。在此,我们将对维吉尔的《牧歌》予以特别的关注;它横跨整片田园诗境,近至空无深意的纯美,远及一幕美丽新世界的轮廓。

2

就像在鉴赏忒奥克里图斯的田园诗时一样,对于古希腊"前人之作"的审视也将有助于我们对维吉尔作品的鉴赏,因为忒式田园诗赖以形成的元素正是通过忒式田园诗本身被导入了维吉尔的创作之中。一切体裁的拉丁诗歌都完全服从古希腊诗歌所确立的标准,以至于罗马诗人只需率先在创作中将某种特定的希腊诗歌形式引入拉丁语世界,便可声称自己的作品出自原创。在古希腊文学中,最为罗马人所熟悉的，莫过于在时间上、性情上都与罗马文学最为接近的亚历山大文学，但一些独具慧眼的作者，比如贺拉斯[22]，也曾转而深入古典时期，为其最杰出的作品寻找模型。随着艺术创作的推进，维吉尔也同样走上了回归古典的道路。在《埃涅阿斯纪》(*Aeneid*)——他最后的也是最伟大的作品中，他不仅采用了富于情爱抑或戏剧性的素材（比如借自亚历山大时代诗人阿波罗尼俄斯的狄朵和埃涅阿斯的爱情悲剧），更在诗歌形式上直接效仿了荷马本人。除了《维吉尔附录》(*Virgilian Appendix*)中那些可疑的少年时代作品之外，《牧歌》是维吉尔最早期的作品，整部诗集都是对忒奥克里图斯的公然模仿。

《牧歌》中的数首诗作都发源于维吉尔创作生涯中的某一特殊事件，这些诗篇的问世对其作品的后续发展造成了极为深远的影响。因此，我们理应对诗人一生的轮廓略加审视。公元前70年10月15日，维吉尔出生在罗马共和国山南高卢行省（Cisalpine Gaul）曼图亚地区（Mantua）附近的一座名叫安德斯（Andes）的小镇，他的父亲是一位富裕的农户。维吉尔少时曾被送到克雷莫纳（Cremona）和米兰的学校念书，后来又到那不勒斯和罗马学习希腊文学、修辞学以及伊壁鸠鲁哲学。在乡村地区度过的幼年时代足以解释他对乡村风土人情与各行各业的深刻理解与丰富知识；这份理解与知识先在《牧歌》中得到了反映，后又成为《农事诗》(*Georgics*)的实质。他在生涯早期对于伊壁鸠鲁学说的认同在他笔下的诸多章节里都得到了体现；"洞悉事物真理的人无比幸福"（《农事诗》第2卷第489行，原文为"Felix qui potuit rerum cognoscere causas"）——如此诗行正是对于伊壁鸠鲁学派在罗马共和国的先驱卢克莱修[23]的直白引用。不过，因为否定神圣关怀在人类事务中起到的作用，伊壁鸠鲁学说也对宗教制裁这一独裁统治的正当理由提出了质疑。所以，在罗马帝国初期，这种学说其实并不受统治阶层待见。

然而，《埃涅阿斯纪》——维吉尔最成熟、最深邃的作品——

却或许可以被相当准确地描述成一份以宗教制裁为基础，以奥古斯都的独裁主义为对象的庄严辩护。最终成长为现有体制支持者的年轻激进分子比比皆是，归附奥古斯都元首统治的人也不应受到真诚与否的质问；直至今日，也没有任何一位政治理论家，能明确指出其他能为罗马共和国末期的政治混乱与血腥内战画上句点的可行办法。不过，话虽如此，事实就是事实：正是在那个年纪轻轻却精明无比，最终成为奥古斯都的屋大维授予他特权之后，维吉尔才开始发声，为元首政治进行辩护。

具体情形如下：布鲁特斯（Brutus）和卡西乌斯（Cassius）于公元前42年在腓立比（Phillipi）战败之后，国家大权完全落入以屋大维为首的"三执政"[24]之手。他们早已承诺将牧场作为奖赏分给麾下军士，而维吉尔的父亲正是因此而被剥夺土地的农户之一。当时，维吉尔的早期诗歌创作（也许就是这部《牧歌》中的一些诗篇）已经引起时任山南高卢行省总督，同时也是一位学者、诗人的阿西尼乌斯·波利奥[25]的兴趣，而波利奥又极力为维吉尔的诗歌争取到了屋大维的关注。结果，维吉尔家的牧场失而复得，维吉尔本人也成了梅塞纳斯[26]（当时的梅塞纳斯实际上就是屋大维的公关大臣）的门客。

正是在梅塞纳斯的请求下，维吉尔创作了四卷旨在传扬意大利受天眷顾的特殊优越性，促进国民回归农业生产与传统的罗马式生活方式的《农事诗》。也正是在梅塞纳斯的建议下，他写下了旨在展现罗马帝国是注定统治世界的天选之国，奥古斯都是奉命引领国家命运的天选之王的《埃涅阿斯纪》。曾在数个章节中满怀情意地提及维吉尔的贺拉斯，正是在维吉尔的引介下结识了梅塞纳斯，后又在以梅塞纳斯为主导的艺术圈内发挥重要影响，成为实际意义上的桂冠诗人。

公元前19年，在与奥古斯都一道从希腊回国途中，维吉尔染上恶疾，于9月22日在布林迪西（Brundisium）逝世。

3

正是在《牧歌》中，我们看见一个年轻的乡村诗人如何蜕变成帝国顶层艺术圈里的名士，一个毫无避讳的效仿者如何蜕变成一位找到属于自己的声音的艺术家。《牧歌》包含十首诗作，它们似乎都创作于公元前 42 年到前 39 年之间，当时的维吉尔年仅三十上下。这十首作品大概的时间顺序，部分可以结合它们对于忒式田园诗模型的依赖程度以及致献对象的不同来判定。《牧歌》其二、其三、其五、其七均为纯粹的模仿，因此无疑是最先成诗的四首，而且成诗顺序很有可能一如编号所示。《牧歌》其四、其八都是写给波利奥的作品，与波利奥的执政官生涯以及他在与帕提尼人（Parthini）的战争中取得的胜利相关的内容，表明二者分别成诗于公元前 40 年与前 39 年，而与失而复得的维家牧场相关的《牧歌》其六、其九则是写给山南高卢行省总督——波利奥的继任者阿尔菲努斯·瓦鲁斯（Alfenus Varus）的作品。最后，献给好友迦鲁斯[27]的《牧歌》其十的篇首一词[28]明确宣告该诗为全集末篇；不过无疑，真正的"全集末篇"当属写给罗马帝国皇帝，旨在将整部诗集献给他的《牧歌》其一。

接着，我们按照传统的编号顺序对这十首牧歌进行简要的概括与点评。

《牧歌》其一在形式上由两位牧羊人的对话构成：梅利博欧斯（Meliboeus）被赶离自家的牧场，正心灰意冷地赶着垂头丧气的羊群，漫无目的地走在路上，而代表维吉尔本人的提提鲁斯（Tityrus）则在自家的田地上，在心满意足的羊群中悠然憩息，放声歌唱他的阿玛瑞梨（Amaryllis）。面对梅利博欧斯出于好奇而非嫉妒的提问，提提鲁斯答说，他曾到宏伟的城市罗马去争取自由，并在那儿得到一位年轻王者的允诺——"照旧喂你的羊，养你的牛"，他将永远把这位恩人当作真正的神来供奉，年年向他献祭，而这命运的转变恰恰发生在他挣脱伽拉忒亚（Galatea）的束缚，将爱意转向阿玛瑞梨之后。接着，梅利博欧斯痛诉自己耗尽心血辛勤耕耘的故土家园丧于异族蛮夷之手，哀叹自己流亡他乡的命运，提提鲁斯殷勤以待，邀他留下歇息一夜。

从表面看来，这是一首诗人借以表达感激之情的诗作，诗文或许有些"过度"，却始终与形式相称，不失为一首完美的传统田园牧歌；一切俱在：纯粹的牧歌式背景，虑乡野之人所虑、为乡野之人所为的对话双方（特别是他们对于大城奇观的惊叹）以及诗人在诗中披上的伪装。提提鲁斯之所以被认作维吉尔本人的写照，仅仅是因为事实上一座充公的牧场已被归还于他，而非因为他表现出任何一种具体的心理特征。梅利博欧斯也完全有可能代表着某一真实存在的人物；他惨遭不公，境况极糟，而他对于提提鲁斯口中那位随口一言便让提家农地失而复得的"神"并无半句反诘这一事实，又让这份"不公"更显尖锐。被抛弃的伽拉忒亚和取而代之的阿玛瑞梨，或许无非就是两个常为诗歌中的牧羊人担任配角的乡村姑娘，但提提鲁斯的弃迦迎阿之举却为他带来了富足——尽管心地纯良的梅利博欧斯所遭遇的不幸让这份富足蒙上了一层淡淡的阴影。也许，维吉尔的爱意并不仅仅是从一个姑娘转移到了另一个姑娘身上。倘若维吉尔的原意果真仅限于男女之间的情变，那么他在被他奉为新神的年轻人面前所表现出来的谦卑之中，便少不了一份苦涩。在他立下誓言，说除非野兽展翅、海鱼学步，他对神的忠诚绝不动摇之际，他所选用的，仅仅是一种被古希腊修辞学家称为"adynata"（意即"不可能的事物"）的标准喻体，但在帕提亚人和高卢人易地而居、换河饮水这一说法之中，恐怕还隐藏着更深层的用意。很有可能，维吉尔意欲传达的，全如诗文表面所示，但另一种可能依然存在，我们无法置之不理：《牧歌》其一或许恰是一席情真意切、直指世间不公的谴责，一份满含苦涩，直斥卑躬屈膝、委曲求全的自我控诉。传风煽火的粗俗之辈必须纵声咆哮，但诗人所言却无须如此明了。

《牧歌》其二或许是诗集中最早成诗的一首。诗中，牧羊人柯吕东（Corydon）因为无法赢得主人家年轻俊俏的男奴阿列克西（Alexis）的芳心而哀叹连连。整首诗作都以忒奥克里图斯田园诗第十一为原型，忒诗中的海洋女仙伽拉忒亚与粗野而可悲、苦恋伽拉忒亚无果的独眼巨人波吕斐摩斯（Polyphemus）分别为阿列克西与柯吕东所置换。一如忒诗中的情形，在《牧歌》其二中，沮丧的求爱者柯吕东讲起他如何全情投入，爱得忘我，强调他拥有的财富，声辩水中的映像证明他的相貌并不丑陋。但除此之外，柯吕东还对自己的唱功有所夸耀；倘若阿列克西终于心软，柯吕东必将把自己的音乐和他分享，尽管一个名叫赛斯提丽（Thestylis）的姑娘渴望与他相爱。城里人的确更受帕拉斯（Pallas，即智慧女神雅典娜）的青睐，但乡下人也有他们自己的守护神。如果这首牧歌仅仅是一次模仿，那么我们必须承认，它远比它的模仿对象逊色。在维吉尔笔下，没有孩子气的巨人，没有美丽的仙女，也没有茫茫海境般迷人的背景，漂亮男孩对于海中女仙的置换更是进一步"败坏"了原作。然而，我们有理由认为，柯吕东或许代表着维吉尔本人；倘若柯吕东的形象也是一层伪装，那么诗中其他形象的真实身份或许也能得到辨认，一出承载着澎湃情感的戏剧或许也会就此蜕去以田园牧歌的传统原料织成的外衣，露出原来的面貌。

《牧歌》其三在很大程度上改编自忒奥克里图斯田园诗第四、第五，很有可能也是成诗时间较早的一首。前六十行诗中，牧羊人梅纳喀斯（Menalcas）和达摩埃塔（Damoetas）先是互致谩骂，后又决定请帕雷蒙（Palaemon）做裁判，以一头奶牛和两只精美的木杯为赌注，展开一场诗歌比赛。之后的四十余行诗中，参赛二人轮流吟唱"对话体"（amoebaean，或称"交互体"）诗文，在裁判宣布二人难分高下之后，全诗结束。这类唱诗比赛似是一种深受牧羊人喜爱的消遣，对于隐藏在面具背后的种种面目和诗文之下的种种深意，即便它们或许真的存在，我们也无须予以深究。

既名"波利奥"，也更常被人称作"弥赛亚牧歌"的《牧歌》其四，远比其他九首作品更为知名。从君士坦丁一世（Constantine）和尤西比乌斯（Eusebius）的时代开始，直到十九世纪，诗中对于一位"先必终结黑铁时代，为广阔世界带来金色黎明的婴孩"即将降世的预言，始终被理解成耶稣降世的预言，而维吉尔之所以能在西方基督教徒的心目中享有近乎圣人一般的威望，正是因为人们相信他确确实实预知到了耶稣的诞生。亚历山大·蒲柏[29]在他的诗作《弥赛亚》（*Messiah*）中效仿了《牧歌》其四，并称《弥赛亚》是"一首效仿维吉尔的'波利奥'而作的神圣牧歌"。为了寻找维吉尔的"天启"之思以及相关表述的来源，现代学者们翻遍了东地中海地区的每一个角落，但实际上，我们只需追溯至《以赛亚书》（*Isaiah*），就能找到其本源。全诗第三行出现的女巫（Sybil）直接指向（依然存世的）《预言书》（*Sibylline Oracles*），而《预言书》的卷三、卷四、卷五无疑都植根于犹太教或者基督教思想。于是，意在描绘历史命运皆由上天注定，历史进程皆由上天委托罗马帝国以及帝国的统治者掌控的《牧歌》其四，实际上就成了一份为《埃涅阿斯纪》而准备的蓝图。

这个一旦降生就将为世界带来崭新秩序的孩子究竟是谁，至今尚无定论。最早的推测是，他是波利奥即将出生的孩子，但屋大维的孩子（虽然出生后才知道是个女孩，而且长大后非常淘气）也是可能的候选。除了鲜花、果实、安宁的家畜和对于航海与贸易的反对之外，这首"更庄重的歌谣"里并没有多少传统田园诗的元素，但在贬低世俗世界，想象一种更美好的新秩序时，《牧歌》其四又将田园牧歌的潜能发挥到了极致。

《牧歌》其五是一首对话体诗歌。牧羊人莫普索斯（Mopsus）和梅纳喀斯在诗中比诗赛歌。二十行介绍性对话后，莫普索斯歌挽达夫尼斯[30]之死，梅纳喀斯歌颂达夫尼斯成神。达夫尼斯是田园诗中理想的牧人；在忒奥克里图斯田园诗第一中，提尔西（Thyrsis）就曾歌唱过他的死亡。单从这一角度来看，《牧歌》其五无非是另一次对于忒诗模型的效仿。但极有可能的是，在维吉尔笔下，达夫尼斯其实代表着尤里乌斯·恺撒（Julius Caesar）；如此一来，恺撒的惨死与神化便在诗中得到了呈现。于是，田园诗人的传统技艺再次成为严肃内涵的载体，不再单单是一种新颖的消遣。

《牧歌》其六是维吉尔写给瓦鲁斯的作品。后者继波利奥之后担任山南高卢地区的总督，并曾帮助维吉尔对抗一名据说曾对维吉尔拳脚相加的百夫长，维护他对自家牧场的所有权。全诗开头，诗人便为无法歌颂瓦鲁斯史诗般的功业而致歉：阿波罗已向诗人发出警告，命其但吟田园牧歌。接着，诗文主体部分描述两位牧羊人如何偶遇放纵过后宿醉未醒的山林之神西伦努斯（Silenus），并用他头顶的花环将他牢牢捆住，强迫他开口唱一支歌；山神与野兽应声起舞，连僵挺的橡树也开始摇头晃脑。歌曲的第一部分描述在创世之初，自然元素在茫茫虚空中汇聚、结合，形成宇宙，随着海洋、大地、太阳、云团、草木与禽兽渐次成形，秩序亦脱胎于混沌之中。在全曲结尾部分，他又以歌为述，讲起与一系列具有象征意义的神话人物相关的故事。歌中涉及宇宙起源的内容显然受到了卢克莱修的影响，而与希腊化时代思想关联密切的神话叙述，则开辟出一条直通某种"第一哲学"（first philosophy，也译"太初哲学"）的严肃道路。诗中，除了显而易见的诗性传统之外，在一种真实的惊奇感得以传达之际，亦有真切的诗意闪耀在字里行间。正因如此，田园诗这一诗歌形式明白无疑地成了某种深层内涵的附属，在"附属关系"不那么明白无疑的诗作中，情况也有可能无异于此。

《牧歌》其七借梅利博欧斯之口讲述了一场发生在牧羊人提尔西与柯吕东[31]之间的对话体诗歌比赛，是一首传统的田园牧歌，内含多种仿自数首忒奥克里图斯田园诗的主题元素。它是一首纯粹的田园牧歌，每一行诗都堪为证明，所以我们难以就诗中的"伪装"与象征意义作出任何推测。

《牧歌》其八是为远征伊利里亚（Illyria），大败帕提尼人后凯旋的波利奥而作的诗。它是一首对话体牧歌：先由达蒙讲述爱人妮萨（Nisa）的不贞让他陷入何等悲痛，再由阿尔菲希波（Alphesiboeus）讲述一位没有名字的女性如何勉力施展魔法，将她游浪在外、迟迟不归的爱人达夫尼斯召回自己身边。达蒙在忆及与心爱的姑娘初次相遇的情景之际所吟,或许是整部《牧歌》中最动人的片段。

> Within our orchard-walls I saw thee first,
> A wee child with her mother—(I was sent
> To guide you)—gathering apples wet with dew.
> Ten years and one I scarce had numbered then;
> Could scarce on tiptoe reach the brittle boughs.
> I saw, I fell, I was myself no more.

> 在果园的篱墙边,我第一次与你见面,
> 我被叫去为你领路——那个年幼的你
> 跟在母亲身后,采摘沾满露湿的苹果。
> 那时,我又大了一岁,将将年满十一,
> 踮脚站在地上,刚能够到细软的树梢。
> 我看到你,爱上你,彻底失去了自己。

阿尔菲希波的故事则仿自感人至深的忒奥克里图斯田园诗第二:那个遭人遗弃,对其所施魔法的效力感到绝望,却又必须用尽一切手段挽救自己的姑娘和她满不在乎、不顾后果的勇敢,都在诗中得到了准确而高效、精妙而真切的刻画。到了维吉尔的时代,如此剧情已经成为老套的文学素材,维吉尔的"再加工"似乎无外乎一次熟练的习作。

《牧歌》其九是最饱满,可能也是最早的一首旨在影射维家牧场失而复得的牧歌(《牧歌》其一、其六亦有所涉及)。故事经过反映在两位牧羊人——利西达斯和莫埃利斯(Moeris)——的对话之中。二人在一条乡间道路上相遇:莫埃利斯已被赶出自家的牧场,此时正为新地主卖命,赶着一群羊羔去往城里的集市。利西达斯已经听说（代表维吉尔的）梅纳喀斯凭借他的诗艺保住了莫家所处一带的土地，而莫埃利斯则如实相告，说他自己和梅纳喀斯本人都是虎口余生，差点丢了性命。接着，二人继续行路，时而吟唱梅纳喀斯的一些诗行，比如成段地回忆以下两段：

Varus! thy name, if Mantua still be ours—
(Mantua! to poor Cremona all too near)—

瓦鲁斯！只要曼图亚——和那倒霉的
克雷莫纳紧紧相依的曼图亚——依然
是我们的家，你的名字就会……

和

Daphnis! why watch those old-world planets rise?
Lo! onward marches sacred Cæsar's star,

何以抬头仰观古老星辰的升降？看哪，
达夫尼斯！神裔恺撒之星正冉冉升起……

这一置两位能文善歌的牧羊人于乡野之地，令其于行路之际谈论诗人与诗艺的手法，借自忒奥克里图斯的田园诗第七。

《牧歌》其十是写给科尼利乌斯·迦鲁斯（Cornelius Gallus）的作品。迦鲁斯比维吉尔年长大约四岁，亦被公认为最伟大的罗马诗人之一。他曾效命于屋大维，负责过意大利北部地区的土地分配，后又参加阿克提姆海战，并在战后出任至关重要的首任埃及总督一职。但在埃及总督任上，他因言行失检而铸下大错（何以失检，错有多大，今已不得而知），于公元前26年被迫自杀。或许正是因为这次重大过失让他身败名裂，他的诗作才没能幸存下来。

维吉尔在开篇首句中宣称，这将是他的最后一首牧歌（也许当时，他已着手《农事诗》的创作），全诗旨在安慰痛失其爱吕柯丽丝（Lycoris）的迦鲁斯。《牧歌》其十或许是整部诗集中技巧性最强的一首。同时，它也是诠释纯粹的技巧能够创造何等美感的绝佳案例。直视之下，诗文所描述的，只是一位现役罗马官员如何被一个水性杨花的名媛抛弃，试图予以宽慰的乡野诸神如何细数吕柯丽丝的不贞，他又如何把自己想象成一名抛开尘世愁苦，与仙女共游山中，让"克里特的利箭飞离帕提亚的弯弓"的阿卡迪亚牧人。但松开道德枷锁之后定睛再看，诗文所呈现的，正是一种普遍甚至粗俗的经验；这种经验被艺术之手改造成一个如此精美而别致的世界，以至于一切凡俗之物都无从侵扰。

4

诗歌无法翻译。像《伊利亚特》（*Illiad*）这样一首意境鲜明、故事性强的诗歌还勉强能在另一种语言中站得住脚，因为无论其"原貌"在翻译过程中蒸发几分，其核心的血肉依然能得到足够的保留。即便是像《埃涅阿斯纪》这样一首意境明暗参半、所传甚于所述的叙事诗，也会让翻译难度与译后鉴赏的难度大大增加。换言之，诗人越是坚持自我对于故事本身的掌控，其诗作便越难翻译；抒情诗之所以最难翻译，正是因为它是最具主观性的一种诗歌。品达和贺拉斯的诗歌一经翻译，必然变得怪异、平庸。唯一可行的译法便是，让同时也是一位诗人的译者来创作另一首能够达成相似效果的诗。但如此一来，这首"新诗"的价值便会直接取决于译者在多大程度上改造了原作。

田园诗的高度风格化无疑会给翻译工作带来特殊的困难。译者自主发挥的空间将会受到极大程度的压缩，因为作为田园诗核心的种种技巧必须在译文中得到保留。田园诗的翻译所需要的，并非原创精神，而是对韵律技术和语言技术的纯熟运用，对一种包括古语和方言在内的特殊词汇的精通，以及强大的模仿能力。译者必须像优秀的戏仿诗人那样，在打消自身喜剧意图的同时兑现他的模仿天赋，但对一流诗人而言，这便意味着自我抹杀。正因如此，令人满意的田园古诗译本才如此稀少。

在已经问世的译本中，查尔斯·斯图尔特·卡尔弗利（Charles Stuart Calverley, 1831—1884）的译本当属最佳。卡尔弗利写过大量在当时极受欢迎的谐趣诗。在严肃文学领域，他最重要的贡献即是忒奥克里图斯田园诗的英译；直到今天，他的译本依然极受敬重。本书中的英文版《牧歌》译制于英译忒诗的成功之后，在知名度上也略逊一筹，毕竟就在文学史上的地位而言，《牧歌》难及忒诗。卡尔弗利是一位优秀的学者（他曾就读于剑桥大学基督学院，并在希腊语和拉丁语诗歌竞赛中赢得奖章，后又在基督学院担任研究员），也是一位优秀的诗化艺术家。他清楚地认识到了自身的天赋与局限，选译《牧歌》——而非《埃涅阿斯纪》或者《农事诗》——便是证明，而他的天赋之一，一如《英国名人传记辞典》（*Dictionary of National Biography*）中他名下的条目所言，正是他那"独一无二的模仿能力"，也正是如此天赋，为他赢得了"或许堪称英语世界最佳戏仿诗人"的评价。

导读注释

1 摩西·豪道什(Moses Hadas, 1900—1966), 美国教师、翻译家, 西方古典学界的泰斗级人物。在美国哥伦比亚大学任教期间, 摩西·豪道什为古典文学的考订与翻译作出了卓越的贡献, 他所致力于确立与振兴的古典文学研究方法至今依然盛行。

2 品达(约前 522 或前 518—前 442 或前 438), 古希腊抒情诗人。

3 忒奥克里图斯(Theocritus, 前三世纪上半叶在世), 古希腊诗人, 西方田园诗的创始人。

4 埃庇卡摩斯(Epicharmus, 前 540—前 450), 古希腊喜剧作家、哲学家。

5 索福戎(Sophron, 前 430 年在世), 古希腊喜剧作家。

6 赫伦达斯(Herondas, 约前三世纪在世), 古希腊喜剧作家。

7 阿卡迪亚(Arcadia), 又名"乌托邦", 原为古希腊一地名, 位于伯罗奔尼撒半岛, 后因在古希腊与古罗马的田园诗中被描绘成一个世外桃源而成为世外桃源的代称。

8 阿里斯托芬(Aristophanes, 约前 446—前 385), 古希腊早期喜剧作家, 后文中的"旧喜剧"即指阿里斯托芬以及阿里斯托芬之前的喜剧作家创作的作品。

9 朗格斯(Longus, 二世纪在世), 古希腊诗人。

10 卡利马科斯(Callimachus, 约前 305—前 240), 古希腊诗人、学者。

11 罗德岛人阿波罗尼俄斯(Apollonius of Rhodes, 前三世纪上半叶在世), 古希腊诗人, 因其创作的史诗《阿尔戈英雄纪》而闻名。

12 梭伦(Solon, 约前 638—前 558), 古希腊政治家、诗人。

13 忒奥格尼斯(Theognis, 约前六世纪在世), 古希腊诗人。

14 欧里庇得斯(Euripides, 前 480—前 406), 古希腊剧作家, 与埃斯库罗斯和索福克勒斯并称为古希腊三大悲剧大师。

15 "新喜剧"与前文中的"旧喜剧"对应,指阿里斯托芬之后的喜剧。

16 缪塞俄斯(Musaeus),传说中的神秘诗人,被视作宗教诗歌的创始人。

17 此处的"英雄格"(heroic meter)即指六步格。

18 玛丽·安托瓦内特(Marie Antoinette,1755—1793),法国国王路易十六的王后。

19 彼翁(Bion,约前二世纪在世),古希腊诗人,善于创作牧歌。

20 埃德蒙·斯宾塞(Edmund Spenser,1552—1599),英国诗人,被誉为文艺复兴时期"诗人中的诗人"。

21 约翰·弥尔顿(John Milton,1608—1674),英国诗人、政论家。

22 贺拉斯(Horace,前65—前8),古罗马诗人、批评家,与维吉尔和奥维德并称为古罗马三大诗人。

23 卢克莱修(Lucretius,约前99—前55),古罗马诗人、哲学家,以长诗《物性论》(*De Rerum Natura*)著称。

24 另两人即安东尼(Anthony)与雷必达(Lepidus)。

25 阿西尼乌斯·波利奥(Asinius Pollio,前76—4),古罗马政治家、历史学者,维吉尔的好友,公元前40年任执政官。

26 梅塞纳斯(Maecenas,前70—前8),古罗马外交家、屋大维的重要谋臣,曾保护并提携包括维吉尔与贺拉斯在内的众多诗人、艺术家;他的名字在西方被视作文学艺术赞助者的代名词。

27 迦鲁斯(Gallus,约前69—前26),古罗马诗人、将领,曾出任埃及总督,后因遭到屋大维的猜忌而自杀。

28 牧歌其十的篇首一词为"Extremum",意为"最后"。

29 亚历山大·蒲柏(Alexander Pope,1688—1744),英国诗人、启蒙主义者,英国新古典主义运动的代表人物。

30 达夫尼斯(Daphnis),传说中的牧人歌手,"牧歌"的始祖。他的爱情与死亡是田园牧歌的重要主题之一。

31 原文为"shepherd Thyrsis and goatherd Corydon",意为"绵羊牧人提尔西与山羊牧人柯吕东",译文从简,均称"牧羊人"。

牧 歌
THE ECLOGUES

其一

梅利博欧斯　　提提鲁斯

ECLOGUE I
MELIBŒUS　　TITYRUS

梅　提提鲁斯，你在山毛榉的绿盖下
　　悠然安卧，用那纤细的芦管
　　试奏山野之歌。我们，正要
　　离开故乡，作别我们深爱的田园；

MELIBŒUS　Stretched in the shadow of the broad beech, thou
　　　　　　Rehearsest, Tityrus, on the slender pipe
　　　　　　Thy woodland music. We our fatherland
　　　　　　Are leaving, we must shun the fields we love:

你呢，提提鲁斯，却徜徉浓荫，
　　教山林回响阿玛瑞梨的"美丽"。

提　梅利博欧斯啊，我这安乐逍遥
　　是拜神明所赐：我将永生永世
　　奉他为神，用自家栏中羔羊的血
　　来浸染他的祭坛。你看，多亏了他，
　　我这牛羊才漫步无虞；多亏了他，
　　我才随心所欲，耍弄我的牧笛。

梅　我心中并无妒忌，唯有满满惊奇，
　　整片乡野尽是如此混乱的光景。

         While, Tityrus, thou, at ease amid the shade,
         Bidd'st answering woods call Amaryllis "fair."

TITYRUS O Melibœus! 'Tis a god that made
      For me this holiday: for god I'll aye
      Account him; many a young lamb from my fold
      Shall stain his altar. Thanks to him, my kine
      Range, as thou seest them: thanks to him, I play
      What songs I list upon my shepherd's pipe.

MELIBŒUS For me, I grudge thee not; I marvel much:
      So sore a trouble is in all the land.

看哪，我身心交瘁，却要赶羊而去，
这头怎么也跟不上的，提提鲁斯，
我还得拽着她走；刚在这榛丛里头，
她生下一双幼崽，可这羊群的希望
却被遗弃在光秃秃的岩石之上。
要是脑袋不犯糊涂，我本就应该
时刻记住：天雷劈落，轰裂栎木，
就已预示着这场灾难，裂缝中那
恶鸦的嘶鸣也已发出相同的警告。
可提提鲁斯，那位神明究竟是谁？

提　从前我傻到以为人们口中的罗马

        Lo! feeble I am driving hence my goats—
        Nay dragging, Tityrus, one, and that with pain.
        For, yeaning here amidst the hazel-stems,
        She left her twin kids—on the naked flint
        She left them; and I lost my promised flock.
        This evil, I remember, oftentimes,
        (Had not my wits been wandering,) oaks foretold
        By heaven's hand smitten: oft the wicked crow
        Croaked the same message from the rifted holm.
        —Yet tell me, Tityrus, of this 'God' of thine.

TITYRUS   The city men call Rome my folly deemed

就像我们这的乡镇一样，牧羊人
牵着牛犊羊羔，在那儿来来往往；
就像小狗大狗，小羊大羊，无非
大小有别，又岂知二者不可类同：
那都城罗马高高昂首，雄视万邦，
就像松柏孤拔，睥睨万千杨柳。

梅　　你汲汲造访罗马，是何缘由？

提　　自由，她终于看到了我的无助：
虽然我年已迟暮，每当剃刀划过，
已有雪白的发须飘落，但她仍肯

Was e'en like this of ours, where week by week
We shepherds journey with our weanling flocks.
So whelp to dog, so kid (I knew) to dam
Was likest: and I judged great things by small.
But o'er all cities this so lifts her head,
As doth o'er osiers lithe the cypress tree.

MELIBŒUS　　What made thee then so keen to look on Rome?

TITYRUS　　Freedom: who marked, at last, my helpless state:
Now that a whiter beard than that of yore
Fell from my razor: still she marked, and came

眷顾于我，在伽拉忒亚离我而去，

阿玛瑞梨作主之后，来伴我左右。

伽拉忒亚占据我时，我丝毫不敢

奢望自由，从无发家致富的念头；

不论从圈中拿出多少祭物，不论

我为无良的城镇压出多少鲜酪，

我都从未把沉沉的钱袋拎回家过。

梅　我曾惊讶，阿玛瑞梨，你何以悲伤，

何以连连向天呼唤，这累累的硕果

又是为谁而空挂枝头，提提鲁斯

已经远去！听哪，提提鲁斯，松木、

(All late) to help me—now that all my thought
Is Amaryllis, Galatea gone.
While Galatea's, I despaired, I own,
Of freedom, and of thrift. Though from my farm
Full many a victim stept, though rich the cheese
Pressed for yon thankless city: still my hand
Returned not, heavy with brass pieces, home.

MELIBŒUS　I wondered, Amaryllis, whence that woe,
And those appeals to heav'n: for whom the peach
Hung undisturbed upon the parent tree
Tityrus was gone! Why, Tityrus, pine and rill,

泉水和整片树林都在唤你"回头！"

提　我又有什么办法？我既无力解开
　　奴隶的枷锁，也找不到善神护佑。
　　可梅利博欧斯啊，就在罗马，我
　　见到了那个年轻的王者；一年之中，
　　有一十二天，我的祭坛将为他升烟。
　　"去吧，照旧喂你的羊，养你的牛"，
　　他就这样答应了我无人答应的祈求。

梅　幸运的老人！土地依然归你所有！
　　虽然这遍地秃石和芦苇丛生的泥沼

         And all these copses, cried to thee, "Come home!"

TITYRUS What could I do? I could not step from out
       My bonds; nor meet, save there, with Pow'rs so kind.
       There, Melibœus, I beheld that youth
       For whom each year twelve days my altars smoke.
       Thus answered he my yet unanswered prayer;
       "Feed still, my lads, your kine, and yoke your bulls."

MELIBŒUS Happy old man! Thy lands are yet thine own!
       Lands broad enough for thee, although bare stones

正侵蚀着每一寸沃土,但对你来说,

它已足够广阔。没有异乡的牧草

困扰怀胎的母羊,没有邻近的牧群

捎来恶疾。幸运啊!在熟悉的溪流

和圣洁的泉水边,你可安享阴凉;

在这里,在你家的篱笆那头,依旧

会有翠柳繁花宴享希伯拉[1]的蜜蜂,

依旧会有嗡嗡柔声送你坠身美梦。

在这里,在陡峭的岩壁下,依旧

还会有采摘葡萄的人临风高歌;

你宠爱的鸽子和在榆树顶端

安巢的斑鸠,也都会低吟不休。

And marsh choke every field with reedy mud.

Strange pastures shall not vex thy teeming ewes,

Nor neighbouring flocks shed o'er them rank disease.

Happy old man! Here, by familiar streams

And holy springs, thou'lt catch the leafy cool.

Here, as of old, yon hedge, thy boundary line,

Its willow-buds a feast for Hybla's bees,

Shall with soft whisperings woo thee to thy sleep.

Here, 'neath the tall cliff, shall the vintager

Sing carols to the winds: while all the time

Thy pets, the stockdoves, and the turtles make

Incessantly their moan from aëry elms.

提　是啊，纵使矫捷的牡鹿觅草天空，
　　纵使大海将鱼赤条条地晾上岸头；
　　纵使帕提亚人和高卢人易地而居，
　　换饮阿拉尔河与底格里斯之水，
　　神的容颜也不会从我心中隐退。

梅　而我们却不得不到利比亚去忍受干渴，
　　到斯基泰[2]去四处流浪，到克里特人
　　封堵奥克西斯[3]急流的地方，到不列颠
　　去过与世隔绝的日子。在遥远的未来，
　　我还能否回到故土，再次见到我那
　　茅草盖顶的小屋？能否满怀惊喜地

TITYRUS　　Aye, and for this shall slim stags graze in air,
　　And ocean cast on shore the shrinking fish;
　　For this, each realm by either wandered o'er,
　　Parthians shall Arar drink, or Tigris Gauls;
　　Ere from this memory shall fade that face!

MELIBŒUS　And we the while must thirst on Libya's sands,
　　O'er Scythia roam, and where the Cretan stems
　　The swift Oaxes; or, with Britons, live
　　Shut out from all the world. Shall I e'er see,
　　In far-off years, my fatherland? the turf
　　That roofs my meagre hut? see, wondering last,

见到我那区区几分王国般的田畴?
垦好的良田何以要让粗鲁的军人霸占,
田里的收成何以要让蛮夷享用? 看哪,
世间争斗害苦了谁——我们耕田播种,
谁来一刀全收! 好了, 梅利博欧斯啊,
准备接种梨树, 种些葡萄去吧! 走吧,
羊儿, 走吧, 曾经如此幸福的羊群!
我将不会再在幽幽碧穴中躺卧, 遥遥
望着你们在绿草茵茵的山崖上停留;
我不会再开口歌唱, 不会再领着你们
吃酸苦的柳叶和开满鲜花的苜蓿去咯。

Those few scant cornblades that are realms to me?
What! must rude soldiers hold these fallows trim?
That corn barbarians? See what comes of strife,
Poor people—where we sowed, what hands shall reap!
Now, Melibœus, pr'ythee graft thy pears,
And range thy vines! Nay on, my she-goats, on,
Once happy flock! For never more must I,
Outstretched in some green hollow, watch you hang
From tufted crags, far up: no carols more
I'll sing: nor, shepherded by me, shall ye
Crop the tart willow and the clover-bloom.

提　　不过，就今天一晚，不妨与我同歇，
　　　以绿叶为床。我这儿有松软的栗子、
　　　熟透的苹果，还有大块的奶酪。
　　　你看，远处的炊烟已袅袅升起，
　　　山冈也已投下又深又长的影子。

TITYRUS　　Yet here, this one night, thou may'st rest with me,
　　　Thy bed green branches. Chestnuts soft have I
　　　And mealy apples, and our fill of cheese.
　　　Already, see, the far-off chimneys smoke,
　　　And deeper grow the shadows of the hills.

其二

柯吕东

ECLOGUE II
CORYDON

柯　主家的爱宠可爱俊俏，牧人柯吕东
　　明知是白费心思，却仍热恋难收，
　　只能日复一日，到茂密的榉树林中，
　　独自一人，身披重重阴影，空怀
　　满腔渴慕，向片片丛林和累累山岩
　　不断抛甩他那杂乱无章的词句：

> *CORYDON*　　For one fair face—his master's idol—burned
> 　　　　　　The shepherd Corydon; and hope had none.
> 　　　　　　Day after day he came ('twas all he could)
> 　　　　　　Where, piles of shadow, thick the beeches rose:
> 　　　　　　There, all alone, his unwrought phrases flung,
> 　　　　　　Bootless as passionate, to copse and crag:

"残忍！难道你不曾留意我的歌声，

一点也不可怜我吗？总有一天，

你会要我的命！此刻，就连牛羊

也得寻找凉爽的树荫，绿色的蜥蜴

也得藏身蒺藜；仆女们正捣碎蒜椒，

为下田收割，难挡炎炎酷热的人们

调制气味浓郁的草药。而我却伴着

响彻林间的蝉噪，在这烈日之下，

追寻你的足迹。我还不如去忍受

阿玛瑞梨的脾气和傲气，还不如

去和梅纳喀斯待在一起，虽然

他一身黑皮，没法和你相比。噢，

"Hardhearted! Naught car'st thou for all my songs,

Naught pitiest. I shall die, one day, for thee.

The very cattle court cool shadows now,

Now the green lizard hides beneath the thorn:

And for the reaper, faint with driving heat,

The handmaids mix the garlic-salad strong.

My only mates, the crickets—as I track

'Neath the fierce sun thy steps—make shrill the woods.

Better to endure the passion and the pride

Of Amaryllis: better to endure

Menalcas—dark albeit as thou art fair.

美少年啊，皎白的山楂花也会凋谢，
黝黑的越橘正待采撷，可别太仰赖
你的皙白。你看不上我，从不关心
我从哪儿来，养了多少雪白的山羊，
又存了多少羊乳。整整一千头羔羊
在西西里翠绿的山坡上漫步，鲜乳
也向来充足，无论寒冬还是酷暑。
而且，我不仅能像狄耳刻的安菲翁 [4]
在阿拉钦图山上召唤牛羊时一样
一展歌喉，长得也并不那么丑陋：
昨天，风平浪静的时候，就在海边
我看着自己的脸，那倒影若非谎言，

Put not, oh fair, in difference of hue

Faith overmuch: the white May-blossoms drop

And die; the hyacinth swart, men gather it.

Thy scorn am I: thou ask'st not whence I am,

How rich in snowy flocks, how stored with milk.

O'er Sicily's green hills a thousand lambs

Wander, all mine: my new milk fails me not

In summer or in snow. Then I can sing

All songs Amphion the Dircæan sang,

Piping his flocks from Attic Aracynth.

Nor am I all uncouth. For yesterday,

When winds had laid the seas, I, from the shore,

任你评选，也不逊达夫尼斯的容颜。

美少年啊，只愿你我隐居陋室穷乡，

猎鹿放羊，以那细软的绿枝为鞭，

把群群小羊带回家园，并以我为伴，

像我一样，与潘神[5]赛歌，放声林间！

是潘神最先教会我们，如何用蜂蜡

把芦管粘连；他护佑着牧群与牧人。

不要担心芦管会擦伤你漂亮的嘴唇，

为了练就高超的曲艺，阿敏塔斯

经历过何等艰辛！我那排箫，七管

Beheld my image. Little need I fear

Daphnis, though thou wert judge, or mirrors lie.

—Oh! be content to haunt ungentle fields,

A cottager, with me; bring down the stag,

And with green switch drive home thy flocks of kids:

Like mine, thy woodland songs shall rival Pan's!

—'Twas Pan first taught us reed on reed to fit

With wax: Pan watches herd and herdsman too.

—Nor blush that reeds should chafe thy pretty lip.

What pains Amyntas took, this skill to gain!

I have a pipe—seven stalks of different lengths

长短各异，是达摩埃塔⁶的临终赠礼；

死前他说："我就把它托付给你。"

如此美誉，让那愚蠢的阿敏塔斯

满心妒忌。我追遍了险峻的峡谷，

逮住两只小鹿，身上还有点点斑白，

每天要吸干两次羊乳。全是为你，

我才一再拒绝赛斯提丽的声声央求，

送她就是！反正你看不上我的礼物。

"来吧，美少年啊！看！林中的女仙

为你撷来满篮的百合，水中的精灵

Compose it—which Damœtas gave me once.

Dying he said, "At last 'tis all thine own."

The fool Amyntas heard, and grudged, the praise.

Two fawns moreover (perilous was the gorge

Down which I tracked them!)—dappled still each skin—

Drain daily two ewe-udders; all for thee.

Long Thestylis has cried to make them hers.

Hers be they—since to thee my gifts are dross.

"Be mine, oh fairest! See! for thee the Nymphs

Bear baskets lily-laden: Naiads bright

皑白闪亮，为你采下含苞的罂粟

和淡紫的罗兰，与水仙和郁郁茴香

融合一处，织入肉桂与万千芳草，

更让嫩黑的越橘沾满野菊的金黄；

我会为你摘来软绒如霜的苹果

和从前我的阿玛瑞梨钟爱的山栗。

还有蜡李：得让它们也同享尊荣。

还得有你，月桂，和你身边的香桃：

我会一同摘下，让你俩馨香交融。

啊呸！乡巴佬柯吕东呀！你爱的人

嘲笑你的礼赠；要用礼物决个胜负，

伊奥拉斯[7]又怎么会输。可怜的我呀，

For thee crop poppy-crests and violets pale,

With daffodil and fragrant fennel-bloom:

Then, weaving cassia in and all sweet things,

Soft hyacinth paint with yellow marigold.

Apples I'll bring thee, hoar with tender bloom,

And chestnuts—which my Amaryllis loved,

And waxen plums: let plums too have their day.

And thee I'll pluck, oh bay, and, myrtle, thee

Its neighbour: neighboured thus your sweets shall mix.

—Pooh! Thou'rt a yokel, Corydon. Thy love

Laughs at thy gifts: if gifts must win the day,

Rich is Iolas. What thing have I,

你都干了些啥？任凭呼啸的南风
伤了花朵，狂乱的野猪脏了泉流。

"可傻子，你为何要逃？天上诸神
和达尔丹的帕里斯[8]，都曾入住林间。
就让帕拉斯[9]留在她亲手建造的城堡，
青山绿水是我的家园。凶猛的狮子
追逐着狼，狼追逐着羊，嬉戏的羊
追逐开花的苜蓿，而我只追逐着你：
狮子、狼、羊、我，无不各逐所爱。
你看！那只只耕牛拉着连轭的耕犁
开始回家，西沉的落日洒下余晖，

Poor I, been asking—while the winds and boars
Ran riot in my pools and o'er my flowers?

"—Yet, fool, whom fliest thou? Gods have dwelt in woods,
And Dardan Paris. Citadels let her
Who built them, Pallas, haunt: green woods for me.
Grim lions hunt the wolf, and wolves the kid,
And kids at play the clover-bloom. I hunt
Thee only: each one drawn to what he loves.
See! trailing from their necks the kine bring home
The plough, and, as he sinks, the sun draws out

拉开两倍于牛身的长影。我却依然
爱得煎熬。可爱情它终究难改难了!"

柯吕东啊柯吕东,你真是鬼迷心窍!
葱茏的榆树上,葡萄藤才修了一半,
何不老实一点,多少做些有用的事,
去编个柳筐,织张芦席?就算今天
你遭人鄙弃,明天也会有人爱你。

To twice their length the shadows. Still I burn
With love. For what can end or alter love?"

Thou'rt raving, simply raving, Corydon.
Clings to thy leafy elm thy half-pruned vine.
Why not begin, at least, to plait with twigs
And limber reeds some useful homely thing?
Thou'lt find another love, if scorned by this.

其三

梅纳喀斯　　达摩埃塔　　帕雷蒙

ECLOGUE III

MENALCAS　　DAMŒTAS　　PALÆMON

梅　达摩埃塔，这是谁家的羊？是梅利博欧斯家的吗？

达　不，是埃贡的羊。埃贡托我帮他照看。

MENALCAS　　Whose flock, Damœtas? Melibœus's?

DAMŒTAS　　No, Ægon's. Ægon left it in my care.

梅　真真是可怜至极的羊哪！你们的主人
　　向尼埃拉大献殷勤，唯恐她爱我更多，
　　竟让一个陌生人来半个时辰挤两次奶，
　　挤得你们筋疲力尽，羔子们统统饿坏。

达　出口伤人，还望三思。我们不是不知
　　在哪座庙里，你是跟谁当着山羊的面
　　干的好事，连善良的女仙都笑你无耻。

MENALCAS　　Unluckiest of flocks! Your master courts

　　　　　　Neæra, wondering if she like me more:

　　　　　　Meanwhile a stranger milks you twice an hour,

　　　　　　Saps the flock's strength, and robs the suckling lambs.

DAMŒTAS　　Yet fling more charily such words at men.

　　　　　　You—while the goats looked goatish—we know who,

　　　　　　And in what chapel—(but the kind Nymphs laughed)—

梅　那她们可曾笑我抄着我那卑鄙的镰刀
　　去糟践弥康[10]家的果树和他新种的葡萄？

达　反正她们没笑我在这棵老榉树下折断
　　达夫尼斯的弓箭，因为你这没良心的，
　　就见不得那孩子收到礼物，不想法子
　　欺负他一下呀，你就比死了还要难受。

梅　小偷无赖都如此猖狂，主家可有良方？
　　你这混蛋布下陷阱，想抓达蒙的山羊，
　　惹得狼狗不停叫嚷，莫非我看走了眼？
　　亏得我大喊："放羊的人呢？提提鲁斯，

　　　　　　　MENALCAS　　Then (was it?) when they saw me Micon's shrubs

　　　　　　　　　　　　　　And young vines hacking with my rascally knife?

　　　　　　　DAMŒTAS　　Or when by this old beech you broke the bow

　　　　　　　　　　　　　　And shafts of Daphnis: which you cried to see,

　　　　　　　　　　　　　　You crossgrained lad, first given to the boy;

　　　　　　　　　　　　　　And harm him somehow you must needs, or die.

　　　　　　　MENALCAS　　Where will lords stop, when knaves are come to this?

　　　　　　　　　　　　　　Did not I see you, scoundrel, in a snare

　　　　　　　　　　　　　　Take Damon's goat, Wolf barking all the while?

　　　　　　　　　　　　　　And when I shouted, "Where's he off to? Call,

把羊赶到这来。"你才偷偷躲进草里。

达　是我唱歌唱赢了他，难道他不该认输，
　　把我用我的芦箫赢下的山羊乖乖给我？
　　你可能不知，那头山羊就该归我所有，
　　他明明可以给我，却要说他做不了主。

梅　他输给了你？你哪儿来的像样的排箫？
　　你这个傻瓜不是只会站在那交叉路口，
　　用根尖声的草管胡乱吹些无聊的曲调？

Tityrus, your flock,"—you skulked behind the sedge.

DAMŒTAS　　Beaten in singing, should he have withheld
　　　　　　 The goat my pipe had by its music earned?
　　　　　　 That goat was mine, you mayn't p'r'aps know: and he
　　　　　　 Owned it himself; but said he could not pay.

MENALCAS　　He beat by you? You own a decent pipe?
　　　　　　 Used you not, dunce, to stand at the crossroads,
　　　　　　 Stifling some lean tune in a squeaky straw?

达　好啊，那就比试比试，看谁唱得过谁！
　　我就以这头奶牛为注，你可不能推诿，
　　她养着两只犊子，还能每天下奶两回。
　　说吧，要是输了，你准备拿什么来赔？

梅　我可不敢拿牲口来作赌注，家有老爹，
　　还有个专横跋扈的后母，牲口的数目，
　　他俩一天两回，数得清楚，其中一位
　　连犊子都数。可既然你定要无理取闹，
　　我就拿这榉木杯子来赌；这一双酒杯

DAMŒTAS　Shall we then try in turn what each can do?
I stake yon cow—nay hang not back—she comes
Twice daily to the pail, is suckling twins.
Say what you'll lay.

MENALCAS　　　　　　　　I durst not wager aught
Against you from the flock: for I have at home
A father, I have a tyrant stepmother.
Both count the flock twice daily, one the kids.
But what you'll own far handsomer, I'll stake
(Since you will be so mad) two beechen cups,

雕工精美，出自伟大的阿吉美顿 [11] 之手，

你得承认，它们可远比牲口来的珍贵。

娴熟的刀工下，一根葡萄藤打着浪卷，

与淡淡萝蔓交织缠绕，顺着杯身垂挂。

柔软的藤弯托起杯心二人：一是柯农 [12]；

二是哪位来着？他以杖为杆 [13]，为人类

划分四季，指明何时收割，何时耕种。

那杯子我从未沾唇，是我藏家的宝贝。

达　阿吉美顿同样也曾为我精制两只酒杯。

杯耳上密密麻麻，雕满了柔软的蔷薇，

俄耳甫斯 [14] 衬着身后一片林木居于杯心。

　　　　　　　　The carved work of the great Alcimedon.

　　　　　　　　O'er them the chiseller's skill has traced a vine

　　　　　　　　That drapes with ivy pale her wide-flung curls.

　　　　　　　　Two figures in the centre: Conon one,

　　　　　　　　And—what's that other's name, who'd take a wand

　　　　　　　　And show the nations how the year goes round;

　　　　　　　　When you should reap, when stoop behind the plough?

　　　　　　　　Ne'er yet my lips came near them, safe hid up.

　　　DAMŒTAS　For me two cups the selfsame workman made,

　　　　　　　　And clasped with lissom briar the handles round.

　　　　　　　　Orpheus i' the centre, with the woods behind.

杯子一样从未沾唇，是我藏家的宝贝。
　　　可如果你睁大眼睛，去看看我的奶牛，
　　　就自会明了，谈这区区酒杯何等无聊。

梅　反正今天你跑不了了，你敢向我挑战，
　　我就敢接招。就让帕雷蒙来做个评判，
　　瞧，他说到就到！你就好好听个清楚，
　　什么叫歌，什么叫唱，别再信口雌黄。

达　来，有本事就开口唱吧。我奉陪到底，
　　又岂会畏缩、退让？只是，帕雷蒙啊，
　　比赛可不是闹着玩的，还请用心听好。

　　　　　　　　　　　　Ne'er yet my lips came near them, safe hid up.
　　　　　　　　　　　　—This talk of cups, if on my cow you've fixed
　　　　　　　　　　　　Your eye, is idle.

　　　　　MENALCAS　　　　　　　Nay you'll not this day
　　　　　　　　　　　　Escape me. Name your spot, and I'll be there.
　　　　　　　　　　　　Our umpire be—Palæmon; here he comes!
　　　　　　　　　　　　I'll teach you how to challenge folks to sing.

　　　　　DAMŒTAS　　Come on, if aught is in you. I'm not loth,
　　　　　　　　　　　　I shrink from no man. Only, neighbour, thou
　　　　　　　　　　　　('Tis no small matter) lay this well to heart.

帕　唱吧。此刻，我们的身下是遍地嫩草，
　　田野重染绿意，树木开始发芽，丛林
　　再披青装，又是一年中最美好的时光。
　　达摩埃塔，你先来吧，梅纳喀斯跟上：
　　缪斯女神们喜欢这样你来我往的对唱。

达　我以朱庇特[15]来开头。神充盈世间万物，
　　他行走在大地之上，会侧耳听我歌唱。

梅　福玻斯[16]予我恩宠，神的祭品四时常有，
　　月桂他自情有独钟，风信子姹紫嫣红。

PALÆMON	Say on, since now we sit on softest grass;
	And now buds every field and every tree,
	And woods are green, and passing fair the year.
	Damœtas, lead. Menalcas, follow next.
	Sing verse for verse: such songs the Muses love.
DAMŒTAS	With Jove we open. Jove fills everything,
	He walks the earth, he listens when I sing.
MENALCAS	Me Phœbus loves. I still have offerings meet
	For Phœbus; bay, and hyacinth blushing sweet.

达　伽拉忒亚，泼辣姑娘，冲我丢来苹果，
　　又飞也似的钻进树林，只为把我吸引。

梅　阿敏塔斯，我的火焰，甘愿与我相伴；
　　狗儿们服服帖帖，好似熟识天上明月。

达　谁又能像我一样有心，在高高的树顶，
　　鸽子筑巢之处，找到送给爱人的礼物。

梅　礼物我已送过，区区十颗金色的苹果；
　　果生野树林中，另外那十颗明天就送。

DAMŒTAS　　Me Galatea pelts with fruit, and flies

(Wild girl) to the woods: but first would catch my eyes.

MENALCAS　　Unbid Amyntas comes to me, my flame;

With Delia's self my dogs are not more tame.

DAMŒTAS　　Gifts have I for my fair: who marked but I

The place where doves had built their nest sky-high?

MENALCAS　　I've sent my poor gift, which the wild wood bore,

Ten golden apples. Soon I'll send ten more.

达　伽拉忒亚在我身边，止不住蜜语甜言，
　　风啊风，请把其中一些带到神的耳中。

梅　阿敏塔斯把我放在心底，又有何意义？
　　我以侍仆为伴，他却镇日与猎人同欢。

达　伊奥拉斯，今天是我生日，把菲利斯[17]
　　带来给我。我将宰牛庆收，把你等候。

梅　可菲利斯是我的爱人，同我难舍难分；
　　她将为我哭泣，并欣然作别伊奥拉斯。

DAMŒTAS　　Oft Galatea tells me—what sweet tales!
　　　　　　Waft to the god's ears just a part, ye gales!

MENALCAS　　At heart Amyntas loves me. Yet what then?
　　　　　　He mates with hunters, I with servingmen.

DAMŒTAS　　Send me thy Phyllis, good Iolas, now.
　　　　　　To-day's my birthday. When I slay my cow
　　　　　　To help my harvest—come, and welcome, thou.

MENALCAS　　Phyllis is my love. When we part, she'll cry;
　　　　　　And fain would bid Iolas' self good-bye.

达　羊怕狼嚎，成熟的庄稼害怕雷鸣雨啸；
　　树怕风躁，我最害怕阿玛瑞梨的嘲笑。

梅　雨润青苗，葡萄叶子喂饱断奶的羊羔，
　　柳抚雌羊，阿敏塔斯的脸庞令我痴狂。

达　日神波利奥中意我这平凡质朴的歌谣。
　　缪斯女神，请以肥犊来犒赏我的挚诚。

梅　波利奥亦作新诗，必以如此公牛献之：
　　时时以犄角相争，蹄子咚咚扬起沙尘。

DAMŒTAS　　Wolves kill the flocks, and storms the ripened corn;
　　　　　　And winds the tree; and me a maiden's scorn.

MENALCAS　　Rain is the land's delight, weaned kids' the vine;
　　　　　　Big ewes' lithe willow; and one fair face mine.

DAMŒTAS　　Pollio loves well this homely muse of mine.
　　　　　　For a new votary fat a calf, ye Nine.

MENALCAS　　Pollio makes songs. For him a bull demand,
　　　　　　Who butts, whose hoofs already spurn the sand.

达　波利奥啊，愿爱你的人随你浪迹天涯，
　　蜜露为他流淌，荆棘丛中有肉桂飘香。

梅　让不讨厌巴维的人爱上你梅维[18]的诗文，
　　让他用狐狸下地耕土，挤尽公羊鲜乳。

达　采摘鲜花和野草莓的小孩，快快躲开！
　　潜伏在那草丛中的，是条冰冷的大蛇。

梅　羊儿啊，河岸危险，千万别走得太远；
　　看，那高傲的公羊，正晾晒他的皮裳。

DAMŒTAS　　Who loves thee, Pollio, go where thou art gone.
　　　　　　For him flow honey, thorns sprout cinnamon.

MENALCAS　　Who loathes not Bavius, let him love thy notes,
　　　　　　Mævius:—and yoke the fox, and milk he-goats.

DAMŒTAS　　Flowers and ground-strawberries while your prize ye make,
　　　　　　Cold in the grass—fly hence, lads—lurks the snake.

MENALCAS　　Sheep, banks are treacherous: draw not over-nigh:
　　　　　　See, now the lordly ram his fleece doth dry.

达   提提鲁斯，请把河边的母羊带到那里，
        到时我亲自前去，在泉中为她们沐浴。

梅   孩子们，快计羊群聚集。要是让暑气
        蒸干了乳水，挤奶的力气又将要白费。

达   野豌豆到处都有，我的公牛依然消瘦，
        就像爱情泛滥难收，苦了牧人与牲口。

梅   我的羊羔皮包骨头，可爱情何错之有。
        羊群背后，必有妒忌的目光化作魔咒。

DAMŒTAS   Tityrus, yon she-goats from the river bring.
                        I in due time will wash them at the spring.

MENALCAS   Call, lads, your sheep. Once more our hands, should heat
                          O'ertake the milk, will press in vain the teat.

DAMŒTAS   How rich these vetches, yet how lean my ox.
                        Love kills alike the herdsman and the flocks.

MENALCAS   My lambs—and here love's not in fault, you'll own—
                          Witched by some jealous eye, are skin and bone.

达　你可知，在世上哪里，天空宽仅三臂？
　　回答我，我便敬奉你为伟大的阿波罗。

梅　你可知，在哪里，花上写着王的名字？ [19]
　　答对之后，菲利斯就会彻底归你所有。

帕　如此激烈的争鸣，岂敢妄论孰劣孰优。
　　你们二人，以及所有畏惧爱情的甜头，
　　饱尝爱情之苦的人都该赢得一头奶牛。
　　孩子们，关上水闸，青草已足饮甘流。

DAMŒTAS　Say in what land—and great Apollo be
　　　　　To me—heaven's arch extends just cubits three.

MENALCAS　Say in what lands with kings' names grav'n are grown
　　　　　Flowers—and be Phyllis yours and yours alone.

PALÆMON　Not mine such strife to settle. You have earned
　　　　　A cow, and you: and whoso else shall e'er
　　　　　Shrink from love's sweets or prove his bitterness.
　　　　　Close, lads, the springs. The meads have drunk enough.

其四

ECLOGUE IV

西西里的缪斯，让我们吟唱一支
更庄重的歌谣！低矮的灌木香桃
无法抓住每一个人的心跳。若要
歌唱山林，理当赋予山林以荣耀。

  Muses of Sicily, a loftier song

  Wake we! Some tire of shrubs and myrtles low.

  Are woods our theme? Then princely be the woods.

女巫在歌中预言的末日已经到来，
世纪轮回的铿锵步伐已重新迈开。
处女星归还[20]，萨图恩的王朝[21]再现，
神圣的一代自九天之上降临人间。
请你祝福那个先必终结黑铁时代，
为广阔世界带来金色黎明的婴孩：
圣洁的卢西娜[22]，你的阿波罗——
已君临天下！当他拉开宏伟序幕，
转动岁月的巨轴，你，波利奥啊，
将在崭新的时代成为我们的新主：
你将抹去我们的罪恶留下的印迹，
驱散那笼罩九州大地的无尽恐惧。

Come are those last days that the Sybil sang:

The ages' mighty march begins anew.

Now comes the virgin, Saturn reigns again:

Now from high heaven descends a wondrous race.

Thou on the newborn babe—who first shall end

That age of iron, bid a golden dawn

Upon the broad world—chaste Lucina, smile:

Now thy Apollo reigns. And, Pollio, thou

Shalt be our Prince, when he that grander age

Opens, and onward roll the mighty moons:

Thou, trampling out what prints our crimes have left,

Shalt free the nations from perpetual fear.

他将在祝福之中睁开眼睛，目睹
英雄与神灵合一，并受神的眷顾，
来统治祖先为之开辟的太平乐土。

赤子啊，为你，犹待开垦的土地
将会献上首份庆礼：豆荚与蔷薇
难掩欣喜，春藤与地黄不罢逶迤；
饱食的山羊无须召唤便丰乳而归，
漫步的牛群不再惧怕狮子的暴戾。
致命的毒草枯萎，邪虫恶蟒尽毙，

While he to bliss shall waken; with the Blest

See the Brave mingling, and be seen of them,

Ruling that world o'er which his father's arm shed peace.—

On thee, child, everywhere shall earth, untilled,

Show'r, her first baby-offerings, vagrant stems

Of ivy, foxglove, and gay briar, and bean;

Unbid the goats shall come big-uddered home,

Nor monstrous lions scare the herded kine.

Thy cradle shall be full of pretty flowers:

Die must the serpent, treacherous poison-plants

绚烂的东方玫瑰将如野草般
漫山遍野地怒放在你的摇篮。

不久以后,当你读懂了英雄的颂诗
和父辈的事记,领悟到真正的价值,
层层柔浪般的稻穗将会一天、一天,
渐渐为广袤的原野披上金黄的新衣;
野棘丛中将会挂满赤紫的葡萄,
粗壮的橡树也会淌出汩汩琼浆。
然昔日的余孽仍在,如阴魂般
唆使人类出航犯海,破浪扬帆,
或垒高墙锁邑,或掘长堑为栏。

  Must die; and Syria's roses spring like weeds.

  But, soon as thou canst read of hero-deeds
  Such as thy father wrought, and understand
  What is true worth: the champaign day by day
  Shall grow more yellow with the waving corn;
  From the wild bramble purpling then shall hang
  The grape; and stubborn oaks drop honeydew.
  Yet traces of that guile of elder days
  Shall linger; bidding men tempt seas in ships,
  Gird towns with walls, cleave furrows in the land.

于是，提菲斯重生，阿尔戈巨舰[23]

满载英雄豪杰，驶向全新的战端。

伟大的战士——阿喀琉斯，将手持

更锋利的剑刃，再次兵临特洛伊城。

待你长大成人，获得坚实的力量，

万千船舶将望洋知返，不再远航；

丰饶大地将尽生财富，尽足所求，

令木筏松舟不复来往，不易一物；

田地作别犁锄，葡萄藤作别镰钩，

农夫们将会解开耕牛颈间的轭扣，

羊毛将不再需要各式颜料的印染，

Then a new Tiphys shall arise, to man

New argosies with heroes: then shall be

New wars; and once more shall be bound for Troy,

A mightier Achilles.

     After this,

When thou hast grown and strengthened into man,

The pilot's self shall range the seas no more;

Nor, each land teeming with the wealth of all,

The floating pines exchange their merchandise.

Vines shall not need the pruning-hook, nor earth

The harrow: ploughmen shall unyoke their steers.

Nor then need wool be taught to counterfeit

草场上的羊群将随心所欲，变换
一身柔绒的色彩，时呈浓浓橘黄，
时呈熠熠红紫，低头觅草的羔羊
亦可随时披上红装。莫伊莱[24]女神
三口同声，宣告命运永恒的意志，
谕令纺锤旋转，织就伟大的世纪。
来吧，天之骄子！朱庇特的后裔！
时将至矣！起步迈向至高的光荣！
看哪，大地、海洋和深远的苍穹
尽在你手，这浑圆而笨重的世界
正向你曲躬。这盛世来临的脚步

> This hue and that. At will the meadow ram
> Shall change to saffron, or the gorgeous tints
> Of Tyre, his fair fleece; and the grazing lamb
> At will put crimson on.
>   So grand an age
> Did those three Sisters bid their spindles spin;
> Three, telling with one voice the changeless will of Fate.
> Oh draw—the time is all but present—near
> To thy great glory, cherished child of heaven,
> Jove's mighty progeny! And lo! the world,
> The round and ponderous world, bows down to thee;
> The earth, the ocean-tracts, the depths of heaven.

让万物欢欣鼓舞，只愿暮年恒久，
一息尚有，许我放声吟颂，尽述
你的宏图，让莱纳斯[25]与俄耳甫斯
纵有父母——卡莉欧佩[26]与阿波罗
从旁相助，也无法与我试比歌喉。
纵使潘神与我赛歌一首，阿卡迪亚
来判个胜负，潘神亦将输得心服。
来吧孩子，请以欢颜回报她的笑靥：
怀胎十月，你的母亲已精疲力竭。
来吧孩子，若你不愿为她一展欢颜，
便不配与天神同餐，与神女同眠。

Lo! nature revels in the coming age.

Oh! may the evening of my days last on,

May breath be mine, till I have told thy deeds!

Not Orpheus then, not Linus, shall outsing

Me: though each vaunts his mother or his sire,

Calliopea this, Apollo that.

Let Pan strive with me, Arcady his judge;

Pan, Arcady his judge, shall yield the palm.

Learn, tiny babe, to read a mother's smile:

Already ten long months have wearied her.

Learn, tiny babe. Him, who ne'er knew such smiles,

Nor god nor goddess bids to board or bed.

其五

梅纳喀斯　　莫普索斯

ECLOGUE V
MENALCAS　　MOPSUS

梅　莫普索斯，你善吹笛，我善吟诗，
　　今日有缘相会，又逢榛红榆翠，
　　色影交织，何不在此小坐片时？

MENALCAS　Mopsus, suppose, now two good men have met—
You at flute-blowing, as at verses I—
We sit down here, where elm and hazel mix.

莫　梅纳喀斯，你为长者，我为后辈，
　　长者之命岂敢有违。风吹影曳，
　　可供小歇，岩穴幽幽，岂是空候！
　　瞧，那岩穴上头，有野藤挂绕，
　　绿叶薄薄披覆，竟似帷幔轻柔。

梅　这片山里唯有阿敏塔斯能和你相比。

莫　莫非他的歌声能与福玻斯争个高低？

梅　请开口唱吧，莫普索斯，尽可高歌
　　"菲利斯的爱恋"，"阿尔肯的功德"，

MOPSUS	Menalcas, meet it is that I obey
	Mine elder. Lead, or into shade—that shifts
	At the wind's fancy—or (mayhap the best)
	Into some cave. See here's a cave, o'er which
	A wild vine flings her flimsy foliage.
MENALCAS	On these hills one—Amyntas—vies with you.
MOPSUS	Suppose he thought to outsing Phœbus' self?
MENALCAS	Mopsus, begin. If aught you know of flames
	That Phyllis kindles; aught of Alcon's worth,

抑或"考德鲁的忿怨"[27]，任君挑选。
吃草的羊羔会由提提鲁斯好生照管。

莫　当然，当然，近日我有新歌一支，
　　歌词已刻上榉树的青皮，连调子
　　也已一并注明。且容我唱来你听，
　　之后再请阿敏塔斯来对唱联吟。

梅　在我看来，你更胜阿敏塔斯一筹，
　　一如橄榄的嫩翠更胜杨柳的纤柔，
　　薰衣草的谦卑难比玫瑰的鲜红。
　　何不闲话少说，你我已身在穴中。

         Or Codrus's ill-temper; then begin:
         Tityrus meanwhile will watch the grazing kids.

MOPSUS Aye, I will sing the song which t'other day
       On a green beech's bark I cut; and scored
       The music, as I wrote. Hear that, and bid
       Amyntas vie with me.

MENALCAS   As willow lithe
       Yields to pale olive; as to crimson beds
       Of roses yields the lowly lavender;
       So, to my mind, Amyntas yields to you.
       But, lad, no more: we are within the cave.

莫（唱）　　达夫尼斯惨遭毒手，林中的仙女
　　　　　　潸然泪流。河水与榛丛皆曾目睹：
　　　　　　达母哀恸，紧抱孩子可怜的尸首，
　　　　　　纵声悲呼："残忍的神灵与星宿！"
　　　　　　达夫尼斯，在那些日子，没有谁
　　　　　　再把自家的牛羊带往清冷的溪流，
　　　　　　没有一只四足的牲口肯低头饮水，
　　　　　　把青草塞进口中。荒山野林呼啸，
　　　　　　回响着大漠雄狮为你献上的哀悼。
　　　　　　达夫尼斯，是你教会人们，如何
　　　　　　驭猛虎驾车，歌酒神之歌；是你，
　　　　　　用柔软的嫩叶来包裹坚硬的戈矛。

MOPSUS (*Sings.*)　　The Nymphs wept Daphnis, slain by ruthless death.
　　　　　　Ye, streams and hazels, were their witnesses:
　　　　　　When, clasping tight her son's unhappy corpse,
　　　　　　"Ruthless," the mother cried, "are gods and stars."
　　　　　　None to the cool brooks led in all those days,
　　　　　　Daphnis, his fed flocks: no four-footed thing
　　　　　　Stooped to the pool, or cropped the meadow grass.
　　　　　　How lions of the desert mourned thy death,
　　　　　　Forests and mountains wild proclaim aloud.
　　　　　　'Twas Daphnis taught mankind to yoke in cars
　　　　　　The tiger; lead the winegod's revel on,
　　　　　　And round the tough spear twine the bending leaf.

如葡萄之于青藤，青藤之于绿树，

如稻禾之于沃土，公牛之于家畜：

你是牧人的骄傲！命运把你带走，

牧神与日神也离开了我们的田畴。

我们如过去一般播撒饱满的麦种，

地里却生出根根毒麦和萧萧芦丛，

紫罗兰不复柔美，水仙不再闪耀，

唯有那荒荆遍地，野棘刺利如刀。

牧人啊，达夫尼斯有命：向大地

抛撒绿叶，再用浓荫把清泉遮蔽！

请为他建一座坟，刻上如是墓铭：

Vines are the green wood's glory, grapes the vine's:

The bull the cattle's, and the rich land's corn:

Thou art thy people's. When thou metst thy doom,

Both Pales and Apollo left our fields.

In furrows where we dropped big barley seeds,

Spring now rank darnel and the barren reed:

Not violet soft and shining daffodil,

But thistles rear themselves and sharp-spiked thorn.

Shepherds, strow earth with leaves, and hang the springs

With darkness! Daphnis asks of you such rites;

And raise a tomb, and place this rhyme thereon:

名起林中，闻于天外；以美牧美，
美冠山野，达夫尼斯已长眠于此。

梅　神圣的歌者，你的诗歌于我而言，
　　仿佛困倦时借草为枕的一晌酣眠，
　　仿佛一股恣意奔涌，至甘、至甜，
　　在炎炎暑热之中解我焦渴的清泉。
　　天赋异禀的少年，你的歌喉笛艺
　　皆已比肩尊师，更非我等所能比，
　　但我仍当以蹩脚的唱技和歌以继，
　　将你歌声中的达夫尼斯——也将
　　爱我如你的达夫尼斯举向那星霄。

"Famed in the green woods, famed beyond the skies,
A fair flock's fairer lord, here Daphnis lies."

MENALCAS　　Welcome thy song to me, oh sacred bard,
　　　　　　As, to the weary, sleep upon the grass:
　　　　　　As, in the summer-heat, a bubbling spring
　　　　　　Of sweetest water, that shall slake our thirst.
　　　　　　In song, as on the pipe, thy master's match,
　　　　　　Thou, gifted lad, shalt now our master be.
　　　　　　Yet will I sing in turn, in my poor way,
　　　　　　My song, and raise thy Daphnis to the stars—
　　　　　　Raise Daphnis to the stars. He loved me too.

莫　　世间有何厚礼能与你的歌声相比？
　　　达夫尼斯至善至美，可歌可泣，
　　　斯提米孔²⁸也早已称颂过你的诗艺。

梅（唱）　天堂异土和星辰云霓都在他脚底，
　　　美丽的达夫尼斯满心讶异、惊奇。
　　　山林、田野，皆为之雀跃，潘神、
　　　牧人与德吕亚²⁹众仙，都欢欣不已。
　　　豺狼已不再设伏，羊群觅草无忧，

MOPSUS　　Could aught in my eyes such a boon outweigh?
　　　　　Song-worthy was thy theme: and Stimichon
　　　　　Told me long since of that same lay of thine.

MENALCAS (*Sings.*)　Heaven's unfamiliar floor, and clouds and stars,
　　　　　Fair Daphnis, wondering, sees beneath his feet.
　　　　　Therefore gay revelries fill wood and field,
　　　　　Pan, and the shepherds, and the Dryad maids.
　　　　　Wolves plot not harm to sheep, nor nets to deer;

罗网亦不再铺撒,麋鹿尽情奔游,
只因达夫尼斯仁厚,赐万物自由。
青山高耸云髻,不掩欢喜,昂首
向星辰而歌,岩石林木纵声和应:
"那是神明!梅纳喀斯!看哪——
是神明!"请你赐福于你的子民!
达夫尼斯,看这祭坛四座:两座
是为供奉日神,两座是为你而备。
我将年年敬献鲜奶与香油:两杯
泛沫的鲜奶和两杯最肥美的香油。
我将倾樽倒注希俄斯[30]的如蜜美酒,
以葡萄佳酿助兴宴酬,每逢秋收

Because kind Daphnis makes it holiday.
The unshorn mountains fling their jubilant voice
Up to the stars: the crags and copses shout
Aloud, "A god, Menalcas, lo! a god."
Oh! be thou kind and good unto thine own!
Behold four altars, Daphnis: two for thee,
Two, piled for Phœbus. Thereupon I'll place
Two cups, with new milk foaming, year by year;
Two goblets filled with richest olive-oil:
And, first with much wine making glad the feast—

便寻阴凉，每逢寒冬便就着灶头。

利西亚的埃贡将为我而一展歌喉，

达摩埃塔又将吹响芦笛，以笛声

为阿尔菲希波[31]的萨提尔[32]之舞伴奏。

每当我们向仙女立誓，每当我们

袚除灾邪，净化田畴，你都必受

我们的祀奉。正如野猪流连山头，

鱼儿眷恋溪流，如蜂群喜食香蜜，

蚱蜢好饮清露，你的声名、功绩

与光荣都将永世长存，永垂不朽。

年复一年，牧羊人们将献上誓言，

你将与巴库斯[33]和刻瑞斯[34]一同见证

At the fireside in snowtime, 'neath the trees

In harvest—pour, rare nectar, from the can

The wines of Chios. Lyctian Ægon then

Shall sing me songs, and to Damœtas' pipe

Alphesibœus dance his Satyr-dance.

And this shalt thou lack never: when we pay

The Nymphs our vows, and when we cleanse the fields.

While boars haunt mountain-heights, and fishes streams,

Bees feed on thyme, and grasshoppers on dew,

Thy name, thy needs, thy glory shall abide.

As Bacchus and as Ceres, so shalt thou

Year after year the shepherd's vows receive;

莫　如此动人的歌谣，我该何以为报？
　　连那南风低啸，浪涛拍岸的喧嚣，
　　和那疾流哗哗穿越石谷时的鸣噪，
　　在我听来，都不及你的歌声美妙。

梅　请先容我奉赠手中这副纤脆的芦笛，
　　它曾教我吟唱"达摩埃塔，这是谁家的羊？"
　　和"主家的爱宠可爱俊俏"。

莫　也请你收下这根牧杖。安提根尼 35

So bind him to the letter of his vow.

MOPSUS　　What can I give thee, what, for such a song?
　　　　　Less sweet to me the coming South-wind's sigh,
　　　　　The sea-wave breaking on the shore, the noise
　　　　　Of rivers, rushing through the stony vales.

MENALCAS　First I shall offer you this brittle pipe.
　　　　　This taught me how to sing, "For one fair face";
　　　　　This taught me "Whose flock? Melibœus's?"

MOPSUS　　Take thou this crook; which oft Antigenes

曾连连向我索要；虽然他讨人欢喜，
却从未将它得到。看这铜黄的杖尖
和均匀的杖节，实在是漂亮至极！

Asked—and he then was loveable—in vain;
Brass-tipped and even-knotted—beautiful!

其六

ECLOGUE VI

起初我的缪斯钟爱牧歌式的小巧歌谣；
她隐居山林，并且从未因此感到羞耻。
我曾歌颂枕戈披甲的王侯，但阿波罗
拉住我的耳朵，警告我说："提提鲁斯，
牧人该把羊儿养胖，把诗歌写得瘦小。"

My muse first stooped to trifle, like the Greek's,
In numbers; and, unblushing, dwelt in woods.
I sang embattled kings: but Cynthius plucked
My ear, and warned me: "Tityrus, fat should be
A shepherd's wethers, but his lays thin-drawn."

所以瓦鲁斯啊,既然想讴歌你的成就,
讲述可怕战争的人到处都有,就让我
用纤纤芦管试奏我的乡野小调。尽管
我也是奉命而作,但若真的有人愿意
阅读我的诗篇,真的有人会为之倾倒,
这片片香桃和无边林野都将为你欢唱!

So—for enough and more will strive to tell,

Varus, thy deeds, and pile up grisly wars—

On pipe of straw will I my wood-notes sing:

I sing not all unbid. Yet oh! should one

Smit by great love, should one read this my lay—

没有诗歌能够赢得阿波罗的至高赞赏，
除非诗的首页写着瓦鲁斯，你的名号。

歌唱吧，仙女！——年轻的克罗米斯
和穆纳西勒[36]发现酣睡洞中的西伦努斯：
他宿醉未醒，血脉偾张，一如往常；
头顶的花环滑落身边，笨重的酒杯
以被手指磨光的杯耳为钩挂在一旁。
因这老头常把他俩戏弄，答应唱歌，
却总不开口，他俩便悄悄向他靠近，
以花冠为镣铐，将他牢牢捆在地上。

Then with thee, Varus, shall our myrtle-groves,
And all these copses, ring. Right dearly loves
Phœbus the page that opens with thy name.

On, sisters!
   —Chromis and Mnasylus saw
(Two lads) Silenus in a cave asleep:
As usual, swoln with yesterday's debauch.
Just where it fell his garland lay hard by;
And on worn handle hung his ponderous can.
They—for the old man oft had cheated each
Of promised songs—draw near, and make his wreaths

连埃格勒,那顶顶可爱的水中女仙

也前来助阵,老头刚一睁眼,便用

桑葚的汁液把那一双鬓眉涂得血红。

遭此暗算,老头哈哈大笑,大喊道:

"这五花大绑可还得了!来来,孩子,

快给我松绑,你们的本事我已领教!

要我唱歌,就竖起耳朵,就唱你们

想听的歌;还有她,我也另有奖赏。"

说着他便开口吟唱,只见山神与野兽

都应声起舞,笔挺的橡树也频频点头。

连阿波罗也不曾让帕纳塞斯的山石

欢欣至此,连俄耳甫斯的天籁之声

Fetters to bind him. Ægle makes a third

(Ægle, the loveliest of the Naiad maids)

To back their fears: and, as his eyes unclose,

Paints brow and temples red with mulberry.

He, laughing at the trick, cries, "Wherefore weave

These fetters? Lads, unbind me: 'tis enough

But to have seemed to have me in your power.

Ye ask a song; then listen. You I'll pay

With song: for her I've other meed in store."

And forthwith he begins. Then might you see

Move to the music Faun and forest-beast,

And tall oaks how their heads. Not so delights

也不曾让罗多佩与伊斯马鲁 [37] 感动如斯。

他歌唱土壤、空气、海水与流火之种
在无边无际的茫茫虚空之中完成汇聚，
令鸿蒙初辟，天地始分，年轻的世界
不断生长延伸，变成一个饱满的球体；
接着，大地开始变得坚硬，如牢墙般
囚海神于大海，令世间万物渐次成形，
直到灿烂的日光照亮满怀敬畏的大地，
漫天的祥云从九霄之上降下甘霖——
森林开始萌芽，大地披上绿装，随处

                Parnassus in Apollo: not so charmed
                At Orpheus Rhodope and Ismarus.

                For this he sang: How, drawn from that vast void,
                Gathered the germs of earth and air and sea
                And liquid flame. How the Beginning sprang
                Thence, and the young world waxed into a ball.
                Then Earth, grown harder, walled the sea-god off
                In seas, and slowly took substantial form:
                Till on an awed world dawned the wondrous sun,
                And straight from heaven, by clouds unbroken, fell
                The showers: as woods first bourgeoned, here and there

可见三两野兽游走在没有名字的山冈。
接着他唱到皮拉抛石[38]、萨图恩的统治、
高加索鸷鸟和盗取天火的普罗米修斯，
也唱到水手们在许拉斯[39]失踪的泉水边
呼唤他们的同伴："许拉斯，许拉斯！"
直到整片海岸都阵阵回响着他的名字。
他安慰爱上一头漂亮公牛的帕西法厄[40]，
说要是世上没有这些长着犄角的牲口，
她本该幸福、快乐。噢！不幸的姑娘，
你真是鬼迷心窍！普洛埃图的女儿们[41]
虽然哞哞学牛，漫步田间，却也不曾
屈膝俯身，向那卑贱的畜生觅爱寻欢，

A wild beast wandering over hills unknown.
Of Pyrrha casting stones, and Saturn's reign,
The stolen fire, the eagles of the rock,
He sings: and then, beside what spring last seen,
The sailors called for Hylas—till the shore
All rang with "Hylas," "Hylas":—and consoles
(Happy if horned herds never had been born)
With some fair bullock's love Pasiphae.
Ah! hapless maid! What madness this of thine?
Once a king's daughters made believe to low,
And ranged the leas: but neither stooped to ask
Those base beasts' love: though each had often feared

尽管她们时常会伸手摸摸光嫩的前额，
生怕头上有犄角萌生，而且日夜忐忑，
唯恐颈间扣上犁轭。噢！不幸的姑娘，
你自流落山间，他却时而以花丛为垫，
侧卧雪白的身体，在那暗绿的橡树下
咀嚼淡翠的青草，时而又随牛群游走，
追求心仪的母牛："仙女啊仙女——
狄克特的仙女们[42]，请封闭林间的空地！
只有这样，我才有可能在偶然间发现
那头恣意漫游的白色公牛留下的踪迹！
或是被郁郁青草吸引，或是跟随牛群，
或是被离群的母牛带进我父亲的牛栏！"

To find the ploughman's gear about her neck,

And felt on her smooth brow for budding horns.

Ah! hapless maid! Thou roam'st from hill to hill:

He under some dark oak—his snowy side

Cushioned on hyacinths—chews the pale-green grass,

Or woos some favourite from the herd. "Close, Nymphs,

Dictæan Nymphs, oh close the forest-glades!

If a bull's random footprints by some chance

Should greet me! Lured, may be, by greener grass,

Or in the herd's wake following, vagrant kine

May bring him straight into my father's fold!"

接着他唱到阿塔兰塔停下飞奔的脚步，

凝望着地上的苹果[43]，唱到法厄同姐妹

被涩苦的树苔包裹，化身为拔地而起、

高大纤挺的赤杨[44]，唱到流浪的迦鲁斯

在帕纳塞斯河畔受到缪斯女神的引领，

以区区凡人之身登上了阿奥尼的圣山[45]，

连福玻斯的歌队都全体起立向他致敬，

牧羊人莱纳斯——那位发间缀满闪闪

鲜花与苦芹的神圣歌者朗声对他说道：

"来吧，快收下此笛，它是缪斯的礼赠！

—Then sings he of that maid who paused to gaze

At the charmed apples—and surrounds with moss,

Bitter tree-moss, the daughters of the Sun,

Till up they spring tall alders. —Then he sings

How Gallus, wandering to Parnassus' stream,

A sister led to the Aonian hills,

And, in a mortal's honour, straight uprose

The choir of Phœbus: How that priest of song,

The shepherd Linus, —all his hair with flowers

And bitter parsley shining, —spake to him.

"Take—lo! the Muses give it thee—this pipe.

她们也曾将它赐予那位阿斯克拉老人 [46]：
他奏笛高歌，直到那毅然挺立的花楸
都随之走下山头。此笛在手，你亦可
一展歌喉，歌唱埃俄利亚森林的起源 [47]，
直到阿波罗都愿为它送上至高的礼赞。"

就像这样，他一刻不停地歌唱，唱到
杜里奇的航船如何遭受斯库拉 [48] 的侵扰，
这恶名昭彰的海妖又如何在大洋深处
纵海狗把惊恐的水手们撕咬，也唱到
忒柔斯如何化身为鸟，菲洛墨拉——
这可怜的女子——曾备下了何等宴席、

Once that Ascræan's old: to this would he
Sing till the sturdy mountain-ash came down.
Sing thou on this, whence sprang Æolia's grove,
Till in no wood Apollo glory more."

So on and on he sang: How Nisus, famed
In story, troubled the Dulichian ships;
And in the deep seas bid her sea-dogs rend
The trembling sailors. Tereus' tale he told,
How he was changed: what banquet Philomel,
What present, decked for him: and how she flew

何等佳礼，继而又如何飞向遥遥蛮荒，

并半途回首，盘旋在老家的屋顶之上。[49]

他唱尽了昔日里福玻斯所吟唱的歌谣，

——欧罗塔斯河[50]曾有幸细细聆听，

岸边的月桂也将歌声熟记于心——

不绝于耳的歌声震颤山谷，直抵星霄，

直到黄昏星缓缓爬上满面惆怅的夜空，

发出赶羊回家、清点数目的闪闪信号。

To the far wilderness; and flying paused—
(Poor thing)—to flutter round her ancient home.

All songs which one day Phœbus sang to charmed
Eurotas—and the laurels learnt them off—
He sang. The thrilled vales fling them to the stars
Till Hesper bade them house and count their flocks,
And journeyed all unwelcome up the sky.

其七

梅利博欧斯　　柯吕东　　提尔西

ECLOGUE VII
MELIBŒUS　　CORYDON　　THYRSIS

梅　达夫尼斯刚在飒飒低吟的橡树下安坐，
　　牧人柯吕东与提尔西便各自赶着羊群
　　会合一处；提尔西赶着绵羊，柯吕东
　　赶着多奶的山羊：二者同为乡野牧人，
　　同样正当英年，不仅能歌善乐，亦能

MELIBŒUS　Daphnis was seated 'neath a murmurous oak,
When Corydon and Thyrsis (so it chanced)
Had driv'n their two flocks—one of sheep, and one
Of teeming goats—together: herdsmen both,
Both in life's spring, and able well to sing,

对歌赛乐。那时我也在场,正自培护
我那香桃的幼苗,令其免受风寒之苦,
却发现羊群中领头的那只已不知去向;
我抬头望见达夫尼斯,他也望见了我,
便出声向我喊道:"梅利博欧斯啊,
快来!你的山羊与羔子都安然无恙。
若能忙里偷闲,不妨坐下一同纳凉,
你的牛儿无须召唤,便会穿越草场,
来这儿汲水饮浆。你看这敏吉河畔[51],
芦草纤柔,绕堤沿岸,似长长青带,
神圣的橡树间,有野蜂的嗡鸣传来。"

Or, challenged, to reply. To that same spot
I, guarding my young myrtles from the frost,
Find my goat strayed, the patriarch of the herd:
And straight spy Daphnis. He, espying me
In turn, cries, "Melibœus! hither, quick!
Thy goat, and kids, are safe. And if thou hast
An hour to spare, sit down beneath the shade.
Hither unbid will troop across the leas
The kine to drink: green Mincius fringes here
His banks with delicate bullrush, and a noise
Of wild bees rises from the sacred oak."

这让我如何是好？我可没有阿尔吉贝[52]
或者菲利斯帮我照看刚刚断奶的羊羔，
可战争一触即发——一场宏大的战争！
提柯二人的比赛岂容错过！所以最后，
我还是为了观赛而耽误了自己的营生。
于是，他二人便依照缪斯女神的喜好，
开始依次对唱——柯吕东率先开口，
提尔西紧跟在后——战争就此打响。
（二人开始对唱）

柯　我挚爱的泉中女仙！请让我放声歌唱，
　　　就像考德鲁[53]那样歌唱，他的诗艺歌喉

What could I do? Alcippe I had none,
Nor Phyllis, to shut up my new-weaned lambs:
Then, there was war on foot—a mighty war—
Thyrsis and Corydon!—So in the end
I made my business wait upon their sport.—
So singing verse for verse—that well the Muse
Might mark it—they began their singing match.
Thus Corydon, thus Thyrsis sang in turn.
(They sing.)

CORYDON　"Ye Fountain Nymphs, my loves! Grant me to sing
　　　Like Codrus—next Apollo's rank his lines—

　　　　只逊阿波罗一筹；倘若夙愿无以为偿，
　　　　　　我便将这手中芦笛高挂在那圣松枝头。

提　　牧羊人啊！用常春藤来装扮诗坛新秀，
　　　　　　让妒气撑破考德鲁的肚腹！若他过分
　　　　把我夸奖，就用毛地黄绕我头顶一周，
　　　　　　以免未来的诗圣经不住他的阿谀吹捧。

柯　　狄安娜[54]啊，小弥康为你献上野猪毛颅
　　　　　　和老鹿巨茸。倘若好运今日眷顾于我，
　　　　月神的造像就将以光洁的云石来塑就，
　　　　　　你的纤纤玉踝就将被绛红的靴筒包裹。

　　　　　　　　　　　Or here—if all may scarce do everything—
　　　　　　　　　　　　I'll hang my pipe up on these sacred pines."

　　　THYRSIS　　"Swains! a new minstrel deck with ivy now,
　　　　　　　　　　Till Codrus burst with envy! Or, should he
　　　　　　　　Flatter o'ermuch, twine foxglove o'er my brow,
　　　　　　　　　　Lest his knave's-flattery spoil the bard to be."

　　　CORYDON　　"'To Dian, from young Micon: this boar's head,
　　　　　　　　　　And these broad antlers of a veteran buck.'
　　　　　　　　Full-length in marble—ankle-bound with red
　　　　　　　　　　Buskins—I'll rear her, should to-day bring luck."

提　普利阿普斯 [55]，这些奶与麦饼便是我们
　　　每年的供品：你照看的园圃已近贫瘠。
　　我们尽了绵力以云石为你塑形，只等
　　　新羔壮大了羊群，定会为你再塑金体。

THYRSIS　"Ask but this bowl, Priapus, and this cake
　　　Each year: for poor the garden thou dost keep.
　　Our small means made thee marble: whom we'll make
　　　Of gold, should lambing multiply our sheep."

柯　　海之少女！你比希伯拉香草更香更甜，
　　　　当成群的牛羊披着浓浓暮色饱食而返，
　　　　　　你似常春藤般优雅，似天鹅一般洁白！
　　　　　　若我多少还招你喜欢，就请寻我而来。

提　　嚄！你大可以说我比漂流的海草还贱，
　　　　　　比地上的苦艾还苦，比笤帚还要粗陋，
　　　　倘若这样的一天，我不觉得度日如年！
　　　　　　回吧，吃不够的羊儿，怎能没臊没羞！

柯　　爬满青苔的溪流，温软如梦乡的草坪

CORYDON　　"Maid of the seas! more sweet than Hybla's thyme,
　　　　　　　　Graceful as ivy, white as is the swan!
　　　　　　　　When home the fed flocks wend at evening's prime,
　　　　　　　　Then come—if aught thou car'st for Corydon."

THYRSIS　　"Hark! bitterer than wormwood may I be,
　　　　　　　　Bristling as broom, as drifted sea-weed cheap,
　　　　　　　　If this day seem not a long year to me!
　　　　　　　　Home, home for very shame, my o'er-fed sheep!"

CORYDON　　"Ye mossy rills, and lawns more soft than dreams,

和为尔等披上了淡淡疏影的浓浓绿叶，
请为牛群驱散炎炎暑热——夏日来临，
　　　碧嫩的新芽满缀枝头，一派兴高采烈。

提　　温暖的炉灶，上好的薪柴，我家常燃
　　　熊熊旺火，连那门框门楣、立柱横梁
都被熏得乌黑——谁又在意北风冰寒：
　　　就像狼不怕羊多，急流不怕堤岸一样。

柯　　此处有绿油油的杜松、毛茸茸的山栗：
　　　每一棵树下都有栗子满地，松果颗颗。
万物欢喜不已；可若美丽的阿列克西

      Thinly roofed over by these leaves of green:
      From the great heat—now summer's come, now teems
       The jocund vine with buds—my cattle screen."

THYRSIS "Warm hearth, good faggots, and great fires you'll find
      In my home: black with smoke are all its planks:
    We laugh, who're in it, at the chill north wind,
      As wolves at troops of sheep, mad streams at banks."

CORYDON "Here furry chestnuts rise and juniper:
     Heaped 'neath each tree the fallen apples lie:
    All smiles. But, once let fair Alexis stir

　　　　下山而来，你看，就连溪水都将干涸。

提　大地焦渴难耐，草木枯萎凋零，青藤
　　　　也不再为高高的山峦披上凉爽的阴影；
　　可我爱的姑娘一旦现身，天上的朱神[56]
　　　　必会普降甘霖，让绿意重返片片山林。

柯　阿尔西德[57]最爱白杨，巴库斯最爱葡萄，
　　　　阿波罗最爱月桂，维纳斯[58]她最爱香桃。
　　我爱的姑娘，却只把那丛丛榛叶喜好，
　　　　可她的喜好，便是世上最美丽的珍宝。

From off these hills—and lo! the streams are dry."

THYRSIS   "Thirsts in parched lands and dies the blighted grass;
　　　　Vines lend no shadow to the mountain height;
　　　But groves shall bloom again, when comes my lass;
　　　　And in glad showers Jove descend in might."

CORYDON   "Poplars Alcides likes, and Bacchus vines;
　　　　Fair Venus myrtle, and Apollo bay;
　　　But while to hazel-leaves my love inclines,
　　　　Nor bays nor myrtles greater are than they."

提　树林中有白蜡清婉，园里有松柏常绿，
　　　　水塘边有白杨英挺，山顶有冷杉苍翠。
　　亲爱的利西达斯，你若常来与我相聚，
　　　　一切树木花草，都将臣服于你的甜美。

梅　以上所有我都亲耳听过：我不曾忘记，
　　提尔西虽竭尽全力，却仍以失败收场，
　　从那天起，我便认定了柯吕东的歌喉。

THYRSIS　"Fair in woods ash; and pine on garden-grass:
　　　　　　On tall cliffs fir; by pools the poplar-tree.
　　　　　But if thou come here oft, sweet Lycidas,
　　　　　　Lawn-pine and mountain-ash must yield to thee."

MELIBŒUS　All this I've heard before: remember well
　　　　　　How Thyrsis strove in vain against defeat.
　　　　　　From that day forth 'twas 'Corydon' for me.

其八

达蒙　　阿尔菲希波

ECLOGUE VIII

DAMON　　ALPHESIBŒUS

让我们赞美达蒙与阿尔菲希波的缪斯！
二人对唱之时，牛儿陶醉得忘了吃草，
山猫惊讶得忘了蹦跳，连奔腾的河流
也停下脚步，回头侧耳——所以在此，
让我们赞美达蒙与阿尔菲希波的缪斯！

       Alphesibœus's and Damon's muse—
       Charmed by whose strife the steer forgot to graze;
       Whose notes made lynxes motionless, and bade
       Rivers turn back and listen—sing we next:
       Alphesibœus's and Damon's muse.

不知此刻的你，是正穿越险峻的石峡，
在波澜壮阔的提马乌斯河[59]上乘风破浪，
还是沿着伊利里亚[60]海岸巡航。更不知
要到何时何日，我才能歌颂你的功绩，
弘扬你的诗名——世上只有你的诗艺
能与索翁[61]的悲剧相比。敬请收下这支
自你而始，也必以你为终，而且本即
奉你之邀而作的诗，并将这一缕细萝
绕你额头一周，与胜利者的桂冠交织。

当清冷的夜色刚从天空消退，当晨露
闪耀在青青草丛，接受牧羊人的祝福，

Winn'st thou the crags of great Timavus now,
Or skirtest strands where break Illyrian seas?
I know not. But oh when shall that day dawn
When I may tell thy deeds? give earth thy lays,
That match alone the pomp of Sophocles?
With thee began, with thee shall end, my song:
Accept what thou didst ask; and round thy brow
Twine this poor ivy with thy victor bays.

'Twas at the hour when night's cold shadow scarce
Had left the skies; when, blest by herdsmen, hangs
The dewdrop on the grass; that Damon leaned

达蒙倚着光滑的橄榄木杖，开始歌唱：

达　升起吧，启明星！引领这美好的一天！
　　曾经，我像丈夫一样爱着妮萨[62]，她却
　　不守贞洁，把我蒙骗。尽管神的审判
　　为时已晚，我仍将在生命的最后一刻
　　借这最后的悲歌向天呼唤，以抒愁怨。

　　　　奏响吧，我的牧笛，与我同唱阿卡迪亚之歌！

　　那儿的森林不罢低吟，青松不罢絮语，
　　相思的牧人不罢恋歌，潘神不罢仙曲。

On his smooth olive-staff, and thus began:

DAMON　"Wake, morning star! Prevent warm day, and come!
　　　　While, duped and humbled, I—because I loved
　　　　Nisa with all a husband's love—complain;
　　　　And call the gods (though naught their cognizance
　　　　Availed) at my last hour, a dying man.

　　　　　　Begin, my flute, a song of Arcady.

　　　　"There forests murmur aye, and pines discourse;
　　　　And lovelorn swains, and Pan, who first reclaimed

正是他让纤纤芦管发出了第一声清音。

　　奏响吧，我的牧笛，与我同唱阿卡迪亚之歌！

男欢女爱，又哪有什么不可思议的事？
谁能料到，妮萨爱的，竟是莫普索斯。
假以时日，就连狮鹫也会和母马结合，
我们的子孙亦将目睹，那胆小的母鹿
会和猎犬同饮共沐。去吧，莫普索斯！
去砍些薪柴，燃起火把，将坚果抛撒，
把美丽的妻子带回你家！为你，新郎！
黄昏之星已悄然闪烁在奥伊塔山[63]之上。

From idleness the reed, hath audience there,

Begin, my flute, a song of Arcady.

"Nisa—is aught impossible in love?—
Is given to Mopsus. Griffins next will mate
With mares: our children see the coward deer
Come with the hound to drink. Go, shape the torch,
Mopsus! fling, bridegroom, nuts! Thou lead'st a wife
Home, and o'er Œta peers the evening star.

奏响吧，我的牧笛，与我同唱阿卡迪亚之歌！

真是郎才女貌！嫁给了一位如意郎君，
你便目中无人；在你看来，我的羊群、
牧笛、粗眉、长胡，无一不令你生厌，
天上的神明也无暇顾及人世间的恩怨。

奏响吧，我的牧笛，与我同唱阿卡迪亚之歌！

在果园的篱墙边，我第一次与你见面，
我被叫去为你领路——那个年幼的你
跟在母亲身后，采摘沾满露湿的苹果。

      Begin, my flute, a song of Arcady.

      "Oh, mated with a worthy husband! thou
      Who scorn'st mankind—abhorr'st this pipe, these goats
      Of mine, and shaggy brows, and hanging beard:
      Nor think'st that gods can see what mortals do!

      Begin, my flute, a song of Arcady.

      "Within our orchard-walls I saw thee first,
       A wee child with her mother—(I was sent
       To guide you)—gathering apples wet with dew.

那时，我又大了一岁，将将年满十一，
踮脚站在地上，刚能够到细软的树梢。
我看到你，爱上你，彻底失去了自己。

  奏响吧，我的牧笛，与我同唱阿卡迪亚之歌！

如今，我方知爱 [64] 为何物。坚硬的岩石
是其襁褓，罗多佩、特马洛斯 [65]，抑或
那些遥居非陆彼端的人，才是其父母。
这小小顽童非我族类，全无半点血肉。

  奏响吧，我的牧笛，与我同唱阿卡迪亚之歌！

Ten years and one I scarce had numbered then;
Could scarce on tiptoe reach the brittle boughs.
I saw, I fell, I was myself no more.

  Begin, my flute, a song of Arcady.

"Now know I what love is. On hard rocks born
Tmaros, or Rhodope, or they who dwell
In utmost Africa do father him;
No child of mortal blood or lineage.

  Begin, my flute, a song of Arcady.

正是这小小顽童,让一位母亲[66]的双手

沾满幼子的鲜血。母弑其子岂不可怕?

可同这狡猾的顽童相比,究竟谁才是

铁石心肠?自是一个狡猾,一个可怕!

奏响吧,我的牧笛,与我同唱阿卡迪亚之歌!

"In her son's blood a mother dipped her hands

At fierce love's bidding. Hard was her heart too—

Which harder? her heart or that knavish boy's?

Knavish the boy, and hard was her heart too.

Begin, my flute, a song of Arcady.

就让豺狼转身，速速远离成群的羔羊，
让坚硬的橡树结出金色的苹果，水仙
在那赤杨的枝头开放；让香桃的茎枝
渗出浓浓的琥珀，猫头鹰与天鹅对唱；
就让牧人成为俄耳甫斯，放迹山林的
俄耳甫斯，抑或作伴海豚的阿里翁[67]吧！

　　奏响吧，我的牧笛，与我同唱阿卡迪亚之歌！

就让大地沦为汪洋大海；别了，山林！
我将从那微风吹拂的山巅之上，纵身
投入万顷波涛。这便是我最后的馈赠。

"Now let the wolf first turn and fly the sheep:
Hard oaks bear golden apples: daffodil
Bloom on the alder: and from myrtle-stems
Ooze richest amber. Let owls vie with swans;
And be as Orpheus—Orpheus in the woods,
Arion with the dolphins—every swain.

　　(Begin, my flute, a song of Arcady.)

"And earth become mid-ocean. Woods, farewell!
Down from some breezy mountain height to the waves
I'll fling me. Take this last gift ere I die.

忘却吧,我的牧笛,忘却这首阿卡迪亚之歌!

至此,达蒙唱罢。缪斯女神,请告诉我们
阿尔菲希波如何作答。我们并非无所不能。

阿 拿水过来,用柔软的羊毛把祭坛环绕,
再把丰郁的马鞭草和至纯的乳香焚烧,
如此一来,纵有神灵明鉴,我也或许
能施展魔法。现一切就绪,只待咒语。

呼唤吧,我的咒语,唤达夫尼斯从城里回家!

Unlearn, my flute, the songs of Arcady."

Thus Damon. How the other made reply,
Sing, sisters. Scarce may all do everything.

ALPHESIBŒUS "Fetch water: wreathe yon altar with soft wool:
And burn rich vervain and brave frankincense;
That I may try my lord's clear sense to warp
With dark rites. Naught is lacking save the songs.

Bring, songs, bring Daphnis from the city home.

如歌的咒语能让天上的月亮坠落人间，
女巫的魔咒曾让奥德修斯的船员幻变，[68]
如歌的咒语能让草中的蛇蟒断成数截。

  呼唤吧，我的咒语，唤达夫尼斯从城里回家！

三根线绳，三种颜色——把你的偶像
牢牢捆住，后再领着偶像绕祭坛三周
——天上的神灵只喜单数，不喜双数。

  呼唤吧，我的咒语，唤达夫尼斯从城里回家！

"Songs can bring down the very moon from heaven.
Circe with songs transformed Ulysses' crew.
Songs shall in sunder burst the cold grass snake.

  Bring, songs, bring Daphnis from the city home.

"Three threads about thee, of three several hues,
I twine; and thrice—(odd numbers please the god)—
Carry thy image round the altar-stones.

  Bring, songs, bring Daphnis from the city home.

来，阿玛瑞梨，给三根线绳打三个结，
要边打边念："我正编织爱情的锁链。"

呼唤吧，我的咒语，唤达夫尼斯从城里回家！

只等在这同一团烈焰之中，泥土变硬，
蜂蜡融化，达夫尼斯亦将被真情感化。
撒下麦粉，用沥青把月桂的枯枝烧焦，
我为他受尽煎熬，他也该尝尝这味道。

呼唤吧，我的咒语，唤达夫尼斯从城里回家！

"Weave, Amaryllis, in three knots three hues.
Just weave and say: 'I'm weaving chains of love.'

Bring, songs, bring Daphnis from the city home.

"As this clay hardens, melts this wax, at one
And the same flame: so Daphnis 'neath my love.
Strew meal, and light with pitch the crackling bay.
Daphnis burns me; for Daphnis burn these bays.

Bring, songs, bring Daphnis from the city home.

让他尝尝这相思之苦，像那母牛一样，
为了寻找失去的伴侣，穿越幽薮长林，
终以青草为垫，疲惫而绝望地卧倒在
溪水之滨，直至更深夜静也了无归心。
让他尝尝这相思之苦，我已病重难愈。

  呼唤吧，我的咒语，唤达夫尼斯从城里回家！

地母啊，这些衣服是那负心人的信物；
昔日他赠予我手，今天，我放在门口，
将这铁证交于你手，但愿他还能回头。

"Be his such longing as the heifer feels,
When, faint with seeking her lost mate through copse
And deepest grove, beside some water-brook
In the green grass she sinks in her despair,
Nor cares to yield possession to the night.
Be his such longing: mine no wish to heal.

  Bring, songs, bring Daphnis from the city home.

"Pledges of love, these clothes the traitor once
Bequeathed me. I commit them, Earth, to thee
Here at my threshold. He is bound by these.

呼唤吧，我的咒语，唤达夫尼斯从城里回家！

莫埃利斯从庞图斯[69]为我摘来这些毒草，
庞图斯盛产这些毒草；我曾亲眼见到
莫埃利斯大显神通，靠这草药的魔力
化身为狼，潜入丛林，或从墓穴之中
唤醒亡灵，或将庄稼移至另一片田地。

呼唤吧，我的咒语，唤达夫尼斯从城里回家！

去，阿玛瑞梨，用手抓起地上的灰烬，
撒入一条奔腾的溪流；手要高过头顶，

    Bring, songs, bring Daphnis from the city home.

"These deadly plants great Mœris gave to me,
In Pontus plucked: in Pontus thousands grow.
By their aid have I seen him skulk in woods
A wolf, unsepulchre the buried dead,
And charm to other fields the standing corn.

    Bring, songs, bring Daphnis from the city home.

"Go, Amaryllis, ashes in thy hand:
Throw them—and look not backwards—o'er thy head

万勿转身回头,我将以此来向他逼近:
无论神谕还是咒语,都无法让他动心。

  呼唤吧,我的咒语,唤达夫尼斯从城里回家!

看哪!我稍一迟疑,一束颤动的火光
便紧攫柴薪,在那余烬之中自发燃起。
岂非大吉大利!必有好事将近!——
许拉斯[70]在家门口大叫不已。是真的吗?
难不成我是白日做梦,自己欺骗自己?

  停下吧,我的咒语,达夫尼斯已从城里回家!

      Into a running stream. These next I'll try

      On Daphnis; who regards not gods nor songs.

        Bring, songs, bring Daphnis from the city home.

      "See! While I hesitate, a quivering flame

      Hath clutched the wood, self-issuing from the ash.

      May this mean good! Something—for Hylas too

      Barks at the gate—it must mean. Is it true?

      Or are we lovers dupes of our own dreams?

        Cease, songs, cease. Daphnis comes from the city home!"

其九

利西达斯　莫埃利斯

ECLOGUE IX
LYCIDAS　MŒRIS

利　莫埃利斯，要去哪里，是在进城的路上？

莫　哎！利西达斯，这有生之年，又何曾
　　想象得到，我们的田地会叫外人霸占；
　　不单听得一句"这儿归我，滚吧老农！"

LYCIDAS　　Mœris, on foot? and on the road to town?

MŒRIS　　Oh Lycidas!—we live to tell—how one—
　　　　(Who dreamed of this?)—a stranger—holds our farm,
　　　　And says, "'Tis mine: its ancient lords, begone!"

还免不了皮肉之苦——只怪命运无常！
今日我替他赶羊，但愿城里没人买账。

利　可是我明明听说，从这山势渐趋低缓，
　　开始沿斜坡下滑的地方，到那小溪边
　　老榉树断枝裂干的地方——整片土地
　　都已经被你们的梅纳喀斯用诗歌救下。

莫　听说而已，可别当真。刀枪剑戟丛中，
　　诗歌一无所用，全如一群多多纳鸽子，[71]
　　在天降鹰隼之际不知所措。若非一只
　　乌鸦飞出橡树的裂洞，前来将我拦住，

                      Beaten, cast down—for Chance is lord of all—
                      We send him—bootlessly mayhap—these kids.

LYCIDAS　Yet all, I heard, from where we lose yon hills,
            With gradual bend down-sloping to the brook,
            And those old beeches, broken columns now,
            Had your Menalcas rescued by his songs.

MŒRIS　Thou heardst. Fame said so. But our songs avail,
          Mœris, no more 'mid warspears than, they say,
          Dodona's doves may, when the eagle stoops.
          A boding raven from a rifted oak

让我无论如何，都不可冲动，切不可
再作无谓的争辩，伟大诗人梅纳喀斯
和你眼前的莫埃利斯就都活不到今天。

利　　老天怎能如此把人捉弄！梅纳喀斯啊，
我们真的差一点就失去了你，失去了
你的诗歌给我们带来的慰藉！没了你，
谁来歌颂仙女？谁来向大地抛撒鲜花，
谁来让汩汩清泉披上浓浓的绿荫？噢！
还有，还有那支我从旁偷听，并暗暗
记在心里的歌谣——记得那天，就在
人见人爱的阿玛瑞梨面前，你曾唱道：

                Warned me, by this means or by that to nip

                This strange strife in the bud: or dead were now

                Thy Mœris; dead were great Menalcas too.

LYCIDAS   Could such curse fall on man? Had we so near

                Lost thee, Menalcas, and thy pleasantries?

                Who then would sing the nymphs? Who strow with flowers

                The ground, or train green darkness o'er the springs?

                And oh! that song, which I (saying ne'er a word)

                Copied one day—(while thou wert off to see

                My darling, Amaryllis)—from thy notes:

"提提鲁斯，我去去就来，要记得喂饱
我的山羊；他们吃饱以后，提提鲁斯，
再带他们畅饮水浆，一路上莫要挡着
那头公羊，当心锋利的羊角把你弄伤。"

莫　那首仍未完成的瓦鲁斯之歌岂不更妙？
"瓦鲁斯！只要曼图亚——和那倒霉的
克雷莫纳[72]紧紧相依的曼图亚——依然
是我们的家，你的名字就会被悦耳的
天鹅之歌高高举向星辰，并响彻九霄。"

利　想唱你便尽情地唱！愿科西嘉的紫杉

        "Feed, while I journey but a few short steps,
        Tityrus, my goats: and, Tityrus, when they've fed,
        Lead them to drink: and cross not by the way
        The he-goat's path: his horns are dangerous."

MŒRIS   But that to Varus, that unfinished one!
        "Varus! thy name, if Mantua still be ours—
        (Mantua! to poor Cremona all too near)—
        Shall tuneful swans exalt unto the stars."

LYCIDAS   Begin, if in thee's aught. So may not yews
        Of Cyrnus lure thy bees: so, clover-fed,

不再吸引你的蜂群，愿这遍地的苜蓿
化作浓浓奶浆，充满梅家牛羊的乳房。
缪斯女神也曾赐我歌声，我吟歌奏曲，
成了牧人们口中的诗人——但我岂能
相信他们，会些雕虫小技便自视诗人：
咯咯鹅鸣又岂能和鸿鹄之声相提并论。

莫　　的确，我正翻来覆去，勉力回想——
　　　但愿我能想起那首歌来——利西达斯，
　　　且听我唱，若没记错，此歌亦是不赖。

　　　"来吧，伽拉忒亚！何以在那浪中取乐？

                    Thy cattle teem with milk. Me too the muse
                    Hath made a minstrel: I have songs; and me
                    The swains call "poet." But I heed them not.
                    For scarce yet sing I as the great ones sing,
                    But, a goose, cackle among piping swans.

MŒRIS   Indeed, I am busy turning o'er and o'er—
                 In hopes to recollect it—in my brain
                 A song, and not a mean one, Lycidas.

                 "Come, Galatea! sport'st thou in the waves?

看这儿阳光灿烂，春意盎然；河岸边
　　　百花齐放，色彩斑斓；幽幽岩穴之上
　　　白杨招展，嫩青的藤萝交织如盖——
　　　来吧！让那骇浪惊涛兀自拍击着海岸。"

利　　此外，还另有一歌，你以为如何——
　　　我曾听到你独自一人放歌夏夜；歌词
　　　已在九霄云外，美妙的旋律犹在耳畔。

莫　　"何以抬头仰观古老星辰的升降？看哪，
　　　达夫尼斯！神裔恺撒之星正冉冉升起，
　　　以璀璨的光芒照亮山谷，令谷中五谷

> Here spring is purpling; thick by river-banks
> Bloom the gay flowers; white poplar climbs above
> The caves, and young vines plait a roof between.
> Come! and let mad seas beat against the shore."

LYCIDAS　　What were those lines that once I heard thee sing,
　　　　　　All uncompanioned on a summer night—
　　　　　　I know the music, if I had the words.

MŒRIS　　"Daphnis! why watch those old-world planets rise?
　　　　　Lo! onward marches sacred Cæsar's star,
　　　　　The star that made the valleys laugh with corn,

尽展笑颜，令向阳的山坡之上，葡萄
更添腮红。达夫尼斯，接种你的梨树，
你的子孙后代，将会摘下成熟的果实。"

时光带走一切，我们的回忆都难幸免。
仍记得在儿时的夏天，我的歌声常把
长如一生的白日葬送。如今，人已老，
歌已忘，莫埃利斯之声已丧——恶狼
曾把莫埃利斯窥望。[73] 但这昔日的歌谣
梅纳喀斯仍会为你一次又一次地重唱。

利　　你的推辞竟只让我更添神往——看哪！

        And grapes grow ruddier upon sunny hills.
        Sow, Daphnis, pears, whereof thy sons shall eat."

        —Time carries all—our memories e'en—away.
        Well I remember how my boyish songs
        Would oft outlast the livelong summer day.
        And now they're all forgot. His very voice
        Hath Mœris lost: on Mœris wolves have looked.
        —But oft thou'lt hear them from Menalcas yet.

LYCIDAS   Thy pleas but draw my passion out. And lo!

为了静静听你高歌一曲,无垠的海面
一片默然,就连飒飒轻风也凝神敛息,
罢了絮语。此刻,我们业已行至半途,
抬首已能遥遥望见比亚诺[74]的坟墓——
就在这里,莫埃利斯——在这农夫们
修枝剪叶之处,让我们携手一展歌喉。

All hushed to listen is the wide sea-floor,
And laid the murmurings of the soughing winds.
And now we're half-way there. I can descry
Bianor's grave. Here, Mœris, where the swains
Are raking off the thick leaves, let us sing.

——要是担心黄昏会唤来细雨，细雨
　　浔了路途，不如边走边唱，边唱边走，
　　不但解了旅途闷愁，我也能为你分忧。

莫　莫再劝我，朋友。该先干好眼前的活：
　　待"诗人"[75]返乡，再把最好的歌唱响。

                                        Or, if we fear lest night meanwhile bring up

                                        The rain clouds, singing let us journey on—

                                        (The way will seem less tedious)—journey on

                                        Singing: and I will ease thee of thy load.

MŒRIS   Cease, lad. We'll do what lies before us now:

              Then sing our best, when comes the Master home.

其十

迦鲁斯

ECLOGUE X

GALLUS

阿瑞图萨[76]，请允许我唱好这最后的歌！

此歌献给迦鲁斯——我的朋友，并请

吕柯丽丝[77]亲自吟诵；问世间谁能拒绝

迦鲁斯的请求？只愿你化作一股清流，

潜入西西里的浪涛下时，多丽丝[78]不会

Oh Arethuse, let this last task be mine!

One song—a song Lycoris' self may read—

My Gallus asks: who'd grudge one song to him?

So, when thou slid'st beneath Sicilian seas,

May ne'er salt Doris mix her stream with thine:

让咸苦的洋流侵蚀你的纯澈。开始吧！
在扁鼻子山羊四处觅食嫩叶青草之时，
让我们来述说迦鲁斯为爱心碎的故事，
整片山林都将成为听众，并应声回奏。

水中的仙女们啊，当迦鲁斯痴情难已，
受尽单恋的煎熬，你们身在何处——
是哪片深山，哪座幽谷？既非品都斯[79]
和帕纳塞斯的峰峦令你们驻足，亦非
阿奥尼山的清泉令你们停留。连月桂、
金桃都为他哭泣；当他困卧孤崖之下，
孑然一人，连那松柏苍苍的迈纳鲁斯[80]

Begin: and sing—while yon blunt muzzles search

The underwood—of Gallus torn by love.

We lack not audience: woods take up the notes.

Where were ye, Naiad Nymphs, in grove or glen,

When Gallus died of unrequited love?

Not heights of Pindus or Parnassus, no

Aonian Aganippe kept ye then.

Him e'en the laurels wept and myrtle-groves.

Stretched 'neath the lone cliff, piny Mænalus

和冰冷的吕凯乌斯[81]山岩也曾为他泪流。
羊群站在四周——他们并不嫌弃我们
——神圣的诗人，也请不要嫌弃他们。
阿多尼斯[82]也曾牧羊河畔。牧羊人来了，
懒散的猪倌来了，刚采完冬天的橡子，
浑身湿透了的梅纳喀斯来了——众人
齐声问道："这般相思究竟缘何而起？"
阿波罗来了，也开口劝道："迦鲁斯，
这岂不荒唐？你爱的人早已随人远去，
此刻正自穿越风雪，走过肃杀的营房。"
西伦努斯来了：茴香花和硕大的百合
织就山野的华饰，在他头顶来回摇晃。

And chill Lycæum's stones all wept for him.
The sheep stood round. They think not scorn of us;
And think not scorn, O priest of song, of them.
Sheep fair Adonis fed beside the brooks.
The shepherds came. The lazy herdsmen came.
Came, from the winter acorns dripping-wet,
Menalcas. "Whence," all ask, "this love of thine?"
Apollo came: and, "Art thou mad," he saith,
"Gallus? Thy love, through bristling camps and snows,
Tracks now another's steps." Silvanus came,
Crowned with his woodland glories: to and fro
Rocked the great lilies and the fennel bloom.

潘也来了——阿卡迪亚的潘神！——
我亲眼见到，他面色通红，脸上抹着
朱砂和接骨木的果浆。"够了，够了，"
他对迦鲁斯说，"这凡尘孽缘，爱神
怎会理得，区区两行清泪，怎够动摇
他的铁石心肠，就像草地喝不够水浆，
山羊吃不够绿叶，蜜蜂也闻不够花香。"
可他伤心地答道："阿卡迪亚的朋友！
只请面对群山，唱此一曲！唯独你们
深谙歌咏之道。噢！倘若你们的笛箫，

Pan came, Arcadia's Pan (I have seen him, red

With elder-berries and with cinnabar):

"Is there no end?" quoth he: "Love heeds not this:

Tears sate not cruel Love: nor rills the leas,

Nor the bees clover, nor green boughs the goat."

But he rejoins sad-faced: "Yet sing this song

Upon your hills, Arcadians! none but ye

Can sing. Oh! pleasantly will rest my bones,

终有一天能向世人娓娓述说我的爱恋，
我的尸骨便会欣然长眠。我多么希望
能像你们一样，做那遍地牛羊的守护，
做在葡萄成熟的季节尽情采撷的农夫！
多希望菲利斯这样的姑娘和阿敏塔斯
这样的儿郎，便是我深情的向往——
皮肤黑些又有何妨？风信子浑身黑紫，
紫罗兰光泽冷暗，只愿我与他俩相伴，
同卧青藤之下，杨柳为幔，阿敏塔斯
织起美丽的花环，菲利斯则歌以载欢。
吕柯丽丝，看这柔草密林，冷涧寒泉：
你我本可在此了却华年，任海枯石烂。

If pipe of yours shall one day tell my loves.
Oh! had I been as you are! kept your flocks,
Or gleaned, a vintager, your mellow grapes!
A Phyllis, an Amyntas—whom you will—
Had been my passion—what if he be dark?
Violets are dark and hyacinths are dark.—
And now should we be sitting side by side,
Willows around us and a vine o'erhead,
He carolling, or plucking garlands she.
—Here are cold springs, Lycoris, and soft lawns,
And woods: with thee I'd here decay and die.

今恶战连绵，生灵涂炭，我戎装入伍，
为爱而战，日日以硝烟为伴枕戈待旦，
而你，竟舍我而去，远离故土，独自
把那莱茵冰河与阿尔卑斯的山雪凝盼。
无情的女人，真叫人啧啧惊叹！但愿
寒霜不会冻伤你的肤骨，嶙峋的冰刃
不会划破你的玉足！——罢了，罢了，
我将拿起阿卡迪亚的牧笛，尽情奏响
我为我的哈尔基斯体[83]诗所作的乐曲。
我意已决——我将忍受这份相思之苦，
从此遁入山林，藏身野兽的巢穴之中，
并将我的爱情刻在树上：当树木生长，

Now, for grim war accoutred, all for love,
In the fray's centre I await the foe:
Thou, in a far land—out the very thought!—
Gazest (ah wilful!) upon Alpine snows
And the froz'n Rhine—without me—all alone!
May that frost harm not thee! that jaggèd ice
Cut ne'er thy dainty feet! I'll go, and play
My stores of music—fashioned for the lyre
Of Chalcis—on the pipe of Arcady.
My choice is made. In woods, mid wild beasts' dens,
I'll bear my love, and carve it on the trees:
That with their growth, my loves may grow and grow.

我的爱情也会生长。我将与仙女携手，
在迈纳鲁斯群山之中随心所欲地漫游，
去追猎那身手矫健的野猪：我的猎狗
会将帕特尼山[84]中的空地团团围住——
纵寒风刺骨，亦脚不停步。我已目睹
自己越岭翻山，穿过回声四起的林丛，
笑看克里特的利箭飞离帕提亚的弯弓：[85]

算了吧！区区幻想岂能治愈你的疯癫！
区区凡人的苦痛岂能博得爱神的垂怜！
可惜仙女、歌谣，都已不复予我愉悦，
青青山林——此刻我得再次与你诀别。

Banded with nymphs I'll roam o'er Mænalus,
Or hunt swift boars; and circle with my dogs,
Unrecking of the cold, Parthenia's glades.
Already over crag and ringing grove
I am borne in fancy: laugh as I let loose
The Cretan arrow from the Parthian bow:

Pooh! will this heal thy madness? will that god
Learn mercy from the agonies of men?
'Tis past: again nymphs, music, fail to please.
Again I bid the very woods begone.

我经历的一切都无法将他改变：即便
我在寒冬腊月痛饮赫伯鲁[86]之水；即便
我毅然拔步，陷身色雷斯[87]的霏霏雨雪；
即便当高大的榆树叶落皮枯，我依然
在巨蟹星[88]下把埃塞俄比亚[89]的羊群放牧。
爱情征服一切，也请让我向爱情屈服！"

——圣洁的女神们，请让你们的诗人
尽情唱完这最后的歌：他正安坐于此，
用纤细的芦管编织牧笛；请让迦鲁斯
真正了解此歌的价值！我对他的情意，
就像阳春三月的赤杨一样，每时每刻

No deed of mine can change him: tho' I drink
Hebrus in mid December: tho' I plunge
In snows of Thrace, the dripping winter's snows:
Tho', when the parched bark dies on the tall elm,
'Neath Cancer's star I tend the Æthiop's sheep.
Love's lord of all. Let me too yield to Love."

—Sung are, oh holy ones, your minstrel's songs:
Who sits here framing pipes with slender reed.
In Gallus' eyes will ye enhance their worth:
Gallus—for whom each hour my passion grows,
As swell green alders when the spring is young.

都在成长。我就此起身:浓稠的阴影
——这杜松的阴影祸及清歌,连牛羊
都避之不及。——回家吧,我的羊儿,
吃饱了就回家去吧,黄昏星已经升起。

                          I rise. The shadows are the singer's bane:
                          Baneful the shadow of the juniper.
                          E'en the flocks like not shadow. Go—the star
                          Of morning breaks—go home, my full-fed sheep.

注释

1. 希伯拉（Hybla），西西里岛上的一座小城，以盛产蜂蜜闻名。
2. 斯基泰（Scythia），古地区名，指古代斯基泰人的游牧地域，包括东北欧至中亚的大片土地。
3. 奥克西斯（Oaxes），古河名，具体流域不详。本节中提到的利比亚、斯基泰、不列颠等地，对于当时的罗马人来说都是世上最遥远、最偏僻的地方。
4. 狄耳刻的安菲翁（Amphion the Dircaean），希腊神话中的英雄，因母亲受底比斯（Thebes）王后狄耳刻欺凌而杀之，并自立为底比斯王；狄耳刻死后化作狄耳刻泉，成为底比斯的象征。传说安菲翁精通音律，曾以音乐移动木石，建成底比斯的城墙。少时的他曾与胞弟一起在阿拉钦图山（Attic Aracynth）上放牧。
5. 潘神（Pan），希腊神话中的畜牧之神。
6. 阿敏塔斯（Amyntas）和达摩埃塔（Damoetas）均为虚构的人物。
7. 伊奥拉斯（Iolas），虚构的人物，柯吕东和"爱宠"阿列克西（Alexis）的"主家"。
8. 达尔丹的帕里斯（Dardan Paris），荷马史诗《伊利亚特》中的特洛伊王子，因带走美女海伦而引发十年特洛伊战争。其年少时亦曾在山中放牧。
9. 帕拉斯（Pallas）即雅典的守护神雅典娜，后文中的城堡即指雅典城。
10. 埃贡（Aegon）、尼埃拉（Neaera）和弥康（Micon）均为虚构的人物。
11. 阿吉美顿（Alcimedon）应是一位著名的工匠。
12. 柯农（Conon，约前280—前220），古希腊数学家、天文学家。
13. 这位"以杖为杆"的伟人一说是古希腊天文学家、数学家欧多克索斯（Eudoxus，约前408—前355），一说是古希腊哲学家、科学家阿基米德（Archimedes，约前287—前212）。
14. 俄耳甫斯（Orpheus），希腊神话中的英雄，缪斯之子，能歌善乐的艺术天才。
15. 朱庇特（Jove），罗马神话中的众神之王，相当于希腊神话中的宙斯（Zeus）。

16 福玻斯（Phoebus），太阳神阿波罗的别称。

17 菲利斯（Phyllis），虚构的人物。

18 巴维（Bavius）和梅维（Maevius）是和维吉尔同时代的罗马诗人，二人曾对维吉尔的作品多有诋毁。

19 关于"宽仅三臂的天空"和"写着王的名字的花"这两道谜题的答案，历来众说纷纭，尚无定论。

20 正义女神艾斯特莱雅（Astraea）原本被派到人间审判是非善恶，与人类一起生活在黄金时代，后来在看尽人间丑恶后返回天庭，化作处女星，故"处女星归还"意即正义回到人间。

21 "萨图恩的王朝"指上古黄金时代，萨图恩（Saturn）据说是史上最早的众神之王。

22 卢西娜（Lucina），罗马神话中司掌生育的神后朱诺（Juno）的别名之一。

23 阿尔戈巨舰（Argo）即希腊神话中伊阿宋（Jason）率领众英雄远赴黑海寻找金羊毛时所乘的巨舰，提菲斯（Tiphys）是舰上的掌舵人。

24 莫伊莱女神（Moerae），原文为"three Sisters"，即命运三女神。

25 莱纳斯（Linus），传说中的诗人，阿波罗之子。

26 卡莉欧佩（Calliopea），缪斯之一，相传为俄耳甫斯之母。

27 "菲利斯的爱恋"，"阿尔肯的功德"和"考德鲁的忿怨"均为歌名。

28 斯提米孔（Stimichon），虚构的人物，有学者认为斯提米孔暗指屋大维的亲信梅塞纳斯。

29 德吕亚（Dryad），希腊神话中的树仙，其与水仙那伊阿得斯（Naiads）共称为山林女仙宁芙（Nymph）。

30 希俄斯（Chios），希腊岛屿，位于爱琴海，以盛产葡萄美酒闻名。

31 阿尔菲希波（Alphesiboeus），虚构的人物。

32 萨提尔（Satyr），希腊神话中半人半兽的森林之神，生性好色，尤喜狂欢。

33 巴库斯（Bacchus），酒神狄俄尼索斯（Dionysus）的别名。

34 刻瑞斯（Ceres），罗马神话中的农业女神。

35 安提根尼（Antigenes），虚构的人物。

36 克罗米斯（Chromis）和穆纳西勒（Mnasylus）均是虚构的牧童，后者的名字亦见于荷马史诗《伊利亚特》。

37　帕纳塞斯（Parnassus），希腊山名，阿波罗信仰的发源地之一；罗多佩（Rhodope）和伊斯马鲁（Ismarus）亦为希腊山名，相传为俄耳甫斯的居地。

38　皮拉（Pyrrha），希腊神话中的人物。宙斯为惩罚人类而发灭世洪水，仅皮拉和她的丈夫丢卡利翁（Deucalion）幸存，二人奉神谕向身后抛掷石块，新人类由此诞生。

39　许拉斯（Hylas），金羊毛传说中的美少年，在为同伴取水时为水仙所掳，就此失踪。

40　帕西法厄（Pasiphae）是克里特王米诺斯（Minos）的王后，因米诺斯未能如约向海神波塞冬（Poseidon）献祭而受到牵连，爱上了海神所赐的一头公牛。

41　梯林斯国王普洛埃图（Proetus）的女儿因冒渎天后赫拉（Hera）而受到惩罚，变得精神错乱，认为自己变成了牛。

42　狄克特（Dicte），山名，位于克里特岛。相传宙斯在狄克特山诞生，在山中仙女的抚养下长大。

43　希腊神话中的女猎手阿塔兰塔（Atalanta）答应嫁给在赛跑中战胜她的求婚者，希波墨涅斯（Hippomenes）向阿芙洛狄忒求助，得到三颗金苹果。比赛中，希波墨涅斯丢下苹果，阿塔兰塔因难抵诱惑，停步拾取苹果而落败。

44　太阳神赫利俄斯（Helios）之子法厄同（Phaeton）因私驾太阳马车而被宙斯以雷刑处死，其姊妹日夜为之哭泣，最终变成两株杨树。

45　"阿奥尼的圣山"（Aonian hills）即赫利孔山（Helicon），位于希腊中部维奥蒂亚地区，相传为缪斯女神喜爱的居地之一；阿奥尼人是该地区的原住民，故有"阿奥尼的圣山"之称。

46　"阿斯克拉老人"指古希腊诗人赫西俄德（Hesiod，约前750—前650），其故乡阿斯克拉（Ascra）位于赫利孔山一带。

47　埃俄利亚（Aeolia），地名，位于小亚细亚北部，当地盛行阿波罗崇拜。有学者认为《埃俄利亚森林的起源》本是迦鲁斯创作的一首诗歌。

48　斯库拉（Scylla）是荷马史诗《奥德赛》中的女妖，曾袭扰过奥德修斯的航船；杜里奇（Dulichium）是奥德修斯治下的一座小岛，在诗中借指奥德修斯。

49 色雷斯王忒柔斯（Tereus）强暴妻子普罗克涅（Procne）的妹妹菲洛墨拉（Philomel），并割掉了她的舌头。普罗克涅为替妹妹报仇，杀死了自己的儿子；宴席之上，普洛克涅诱使忒柔斯食子之肉，菲洛墨拉呈上幼子首级，于是忒柔斯拔剑相向，欲斩杀二人，却变成一只戴胜，普罗克涅与菲洛墨拉亦化身为鸟。

50 欧罗塔斯河（Eurotas），希腊南部河流，传说阿波罗曾放歌河畔。

51 敏吉河（Mincius），意大利北部河流，该河流经维吉尔的家乡曼图亚。

52 阿尔吉贝（Alcippe），虚构的人物。

53 考德鲁（Codrus）可能是当时一位有名的诗人。

54 狄安娜（Diana），罗马神话中的月亮与橡树女神。

55 普利阿普斯（Priapus），希腊神话中的生殖之神。罗马人将其雕像置于田间，以吓退盗贼与鸟雀。

56 "朱神"即朱庇特。

57 阿尔西德（Alcides）即希腊神话中力大无穷的英雄赫拉克勒斯（Heracles）。

58 维纳斯（Venus），罗马神话中爱与美的女神，相当于希腊神话中的阿芙洛狄忒。

59 提马乌斯河（Timavus），今名提马沃河（Timavo），发源于斯洛文尼亚境内，注入亚得里亚海。

60 伊利里亚（Illyria），古地区名，位于巴尔干半岛西北部，西临亚得里亚海。

61 "索翁"即古希腊诗人、剧作家索福克勒斯（Sophocles，约前496—前406）。

62 妮萨（Nisa），虚构的人物。

63 奥伊塔山（Oeta），希腊中部山岳，品都斯山的支脉。

64 此处的"爱"指罗马神话中的小爱神丘比特，即后文中的"小小顽童"。

65 特马洛斯（Tmaros），山名，位于希腊西北部，品都斯山脉的组成部分。

66 此处的"母亲"指科尔基斯公主美狄亚（Medea）。她爱上了到科尔基斯寻找金羊毛的伊阿宋，后因伊阿宋另结新欢而在嫉恨之下杀死了她和伊阿宋所生的孩子。

67 阿里翁（Arion，前七世纪在世），古希腊传奇诗人、音乐家，传说他曾在海上遇盗，在绝望之际唱着歌投入海中，被一只迷恋其歌声的海豚救上了岸。

68 荷马史诗《奥德赛》中，女巫喀耳刻（Circe）宴请奥德修斯的船员，在食物中加入魔药，将船员们变成了猪。

69 此处的庞图斯（Pontus）指黑海及其周边地区。

70 此处的"许拉斯"是狗的名字。

71 古希腊历史学家希罗多德（Herodotus，约前484—前425）在其代表作《历史》中记载，在希腊西北部的多多纳（Dodona），一只鸽子用人类的语言宣告了神的旨意，人们奉旨建立了希腊最早的神示所。

72 克雷莫纳，意大利北部城市，位于曼图亚以西。

73 "恶狼的窥望"是古意大利的一种迷信，据说如果一个人在行路途中遇到了狼，并在发现狼之前先被狼看见，他的嗓子就会哑掉。

74 比亚诺（Bianor），据说是曼图亚城的建立者。

75 此处的"诗人"指梅纳喀斯。

76 阿瑞图萨（Arethuse），水中仙女之一。希腊神话中，她在河神阿尔菲俄斯（Alpheus）的追逐下，从希腊越海逃到意大利的西西里岛。本诗中她被奉为牧歌的守护神。

77 吕柯丽丝是迦鲁斯在自己的诗中对其心上人的称谓。

78 多丽丝（Doris），希腊神话中的海洋女神。

79 品都斯山脉（Pindus），希腊主要山脉之一，迪巴拉山脉的延伸，位于巴尔干半岛中部，长约270公里。

80 迈纳鲁斯山（Maenalus），希腊阿卡迪亚地区的山脉。

81 吕凯乌斯山（Lycaeus），希腊阿卡迪亚地区的山岳，相传为潘神的出生地。

82 阿多尼斯，希腊神话中深受爱与美的女神阿芙洛狄忒宠爱的美少年。

83 哈尔基斯（Chalcis）诗体，一般指由出生在埃维亚岛哈尔基斯的古希腊诗人尤弗里翁（Euphorion）所创立的诗体。

84 帕特尼山（Parthenia），希腊阿卡迪亚地区的山脉。

85 帕提亚（Parthia，又名"安息"）帝国与克里特岛古城赛东尼亚（Cydonia）分别以弯弓与利矢闻名。

86 赫伯鲁河（Hebrus），今名马里查河（Maritsa），发源于保加利亚境内，流经希腊与土耳其边境，注入爱琴海。

87　色雷斯地区（Thrace）今指包含希腊北部、保加利亚南部以及土耳其的欧洲部分在内的大片土地；此处的色雷斯泛指寒冷的北方。

88　此处的巨蟹星（Cancer's star）指夏天的烈日。

89　埃塞俄比亚（Aethiopia）是《荷马史诗》中人类无法到达的世界尽头，此处的"埃塞俄比亚"泛指遥远而炎热的南方。